CHARLES R. STURGE
3044 Kaiser Rd. N.W. #3
Olympia, WA 98502

# EMOTIONAL FIRST AID

# EMOTIONAL FIRST AID

*Charles R. Sturge*

An Exposition-Banner Book

**EXPOSITION PRESS**     **NEW YORK**

EXPOSITION PRESS INC.

50 Jericho Turnpike       Jericho, New York 11753

FIRST EDITION

© 1971 by Charles R. Sturge. *All rights reserved, including the right of reproduction in whole or in part in any form except for short quotations in critical essays and reviews.* Manufactured in the United States of America.

LIBRARY OF CONGRESS CATALOG CARD NUMBER: 78-146916

0-682-47219-0

# Contents

1. The Need: To Prevent Unnecessary Suffering ... 9
2. Something Can Be Done ... 15
3. What Is Emotional Health? ... 21
4. The Game of Life ... 26
5. Communication Technology ... 30
6. Care and Feeding of the Body ... 38
7. Havingness ... 46
8. Invalidation ... 49
9. Emotional Shock ... 57
10. Self-image ... 67
11. Control, Freedom, Security ... 72
12. Psycho-cybernetics ... 76
13. Stable Data, Meaningful Truth ... 80
14. Religion ... 87
15. Time ... 101
16. Love ... 106
17. Anger and Healthy Fights ... 113
18. Grief ... 117
19. Successful Learning ... 124
20. Work ... 135
21. Tiredness ... 147
22. Family Counseling ... 151
23. Local Agencies ... 157
24. Real Crises, Symptoms, Civil Disasters ... 159
25. Amateur Counseling ... 164

# EMOTIONAL FIRST AID

CHAPTER 1

# *The Need: To Prevent Unnecessary Suffering*

It is astonishing that neither students, parents nor teachers have a working definition of emotional health. The lack of emotional skills is evident everywhere: run-down neighborhoods, broken homes, poverty, bulging institutions and almost-empty churches.

—20 million persons affected by mental and emotional illness.

—At least as many people are hospitalized with mental illness as with all other diseases combined.

—At least 50 percent of all medical and surgical cases have emotional complications.

—We need twice as many Mental Health clinics.

—There are about 22,000 psychiatrists; we need twice as many—now. Where will they come from?

—Mental illness costs the U.S. about $20 billion a year.\*

People are confused about morality, frustrated about patriotism and searching desperately for a purposeful meaning to life.

In an address to a group of social workers a judge said recently, "Every year I watch broken homes and broken lives come through my court—each one an emotional disaster. Each case is a personal crisis, after months or years of bitter suffering. Courts can't cure these things. Isn't anybody doing anything about *prevention?*"

Case histories tell of long emotional suffering. Where was the beginning? Was it a childhood fear? A deep loneliness? A seemingly unforgivable insult? A failure to live up to one's own standard of excellence? In each case there was an early situation which began the pattern of emotional distress that snowballed into un-

---

\* Data published by National Association for Mental Health, Inc., 10 Columbus Circle, N.Y. 10019.

told suffering. *Prevention* must come by having First Aid available on the spot, at the moment of the initial traumatic situation. Prevention cannot be done by courts, hospitals or crisis clinics. It cannot be done by medical doctors, social workers or psychiatrists. Prevention, if it is to be done at all, will have to be done by yourself, a parent or an ordinary person nearby.

The courts, social workers, and so on, have their own very important role in the big picture. Only they can authorize and sponsor community-wide classes and other educational plans for teaching the public what they need to know to take better care of themselves and their children.

## WHAT IS EMOTIONAL FIRST AID?

Emotional First Aid resembles Red Cross (physical) First Aid. The principles which justify the Red Cross textbook and training courses are equally valid for an Emotional First Aid program.

—Both teach that much suffering can be avoided by not letting it happen; by studying case histories of accidents, studying causes, determining unsafe conditions and practices and finally establishing a militant, determined safety program. Make people safety-conscious. Don't ask for trouble. Watch for potentially dangerous situations. Plan ahead, think. Learn good safety habits.

—Both teach that after accidents and traumatic events do happen, damage can be controlled and kept to a minimum by using approved procedures. Perhaps therapy should commence at once, or professional aid be summoned promptly. There are many sensible things to be done which ordinary people can do if they are confident that they have the simple skills required.

—Special vocabulary and natural principles are taught so that people can observe situations intelligently and discuss them easily. They can make useful reports and ask for and receive help, sometimes by phone or radio.

—The textbook recommends on-the-spot procedures, listing the do's and don't's, based on the wisdom and experience of experts.

## The Need: To Prevent Unnecessary Suffering

—True emergencies requiring prompt professional attention are described.

—Lay practitioners, "First Aiders," are given courses to learn and practice special skills. They are awarded certificates authorizing them to do certain things and to accept certain responsibilities for which they have been trained. Firemen, ambulance drivers, medical corpsmen, practical nurses, lifeguards, youth-camp directors, are illustrations of the principle "Train and authorize."

To summarize: What is First Aid about?

—Common-sense safety.
—On-the-scene help.
—Understanding principles and vocabulary.
—Recognizing true emergencies.
—Training and authorizing responsible citizens.

Procedures and services suggested in this book are not intended to replace psychiatric counseling or therapy when professional services are available. It is hoped that doctors in every community will supervise the First Aid training courses and make themselves available to First Aid practitioners for emergencies and to create opportunities for advanced specialized training.

Far from being an authoritative comprehensive text, this book is a beginning, to prove that something can be done about *prevention* of unnecessary emotional suffering. It is hoped that many able students and instructors will send in additional data, theories, illustrative case histories, cartoons and suggestions for simple practical processes.

### WHO SHOULD STUDY EMOTIONAL FIRST AID?

This book is for ordinary people: teenagers, parents, school-teachers, Sunday-school teachers, scouters, camp counselors, grandmothers. It is also for ministers, lawyers, nurses, policemen, personnel directors, military commanders and social workers—all professional people who must face emotional crises every day, yet are not psychologists or psychiatrists.

The need for universal First Aid training is plainly evident in everyday life. You see children being mistreated by thoughtless parents; frustrated students dropping out of school; marriages breaking up; criminals being sentenced to prison. Every teenager could benefit from annual counseling interviews concerning his attitudes, personal problems, self-image and vocational goals. It has been estimated that one out of ten people will require professional emotional therapy sometime during his lifetime. While reviewing the following list of specialized emotional problems, consider also the fringe area: around each person experiencing a personal problem are others who share his distress emotionally and financially. Many of these problems cause secondary problems. Everyone *needs to know,* for the same reasons we all need to know how to clean a cut and bandage it, to prevent unnecessary suffering.

## SPECIALIZED EMOTIONAL PROBLEMS

The groups listed here have severe emotional problems which deserve the best professional care available. A vast supply of booklets, data sheets and magazine articles is available to instructors and students having special interests in one of these groups. One purpose of this book is to suggest common denominators, common natural laws operating wherever people are in trouble. What do these groups have in common?

—Retarded: people of all ages with subnormal mental and emotional ability.

—Mentally ill: in or out of institutions.

—Institutionalized persons: in prison, POW camps, reform schools, orphanages, and so on.

—Sick people: bedridden, disabled, disfigured.

—Old folks: poor, lonely, unwanted, sick, hopeless.

—Children: delinquents, dropouts, with problem parents.

—Marriage problems: in-laws, divorce.

—Unemployed: anxiety, insecurity, compounded emotional liabilities preventing re-employment.

—Welfare cases.

—Industry: labor-management turmoil; economic disasters.

## The Need: To Prevent Unnecessary Suffering

—Disaster areas: persons in shock, great personal losses, mass confusion, insecurity, need for leadership.

—Minority groups: Indians, Mexicans, Eskimos, and so on, migrant farm workers, "lost" men on skid row.

—Self-improvement seekers: disillusioned, self-critical, confused, hopeless, contemplating suicide.

### OBJECTIONS TO AMATEUR PSYCHIATRISTS

Psychologists and psychiatrists resist and discourage the idea of sponsoring or even permitting amateur counseling. They have several valid reasons:

—There have been quacks—unlicensed, untrained, incompetent—who charged big fees, dispensed dangerous advice and often delayed urgently needed therapy. The public should be protected from them.

—In spite of several years of intense academic training and internship, even the best doctors are often confronted with mystifying symptoms, some of which are violent. The best training is none too much.

—A doctor has the right to do what seems best in an emergency on the basis of his extensive training; a layman could easily do something dangerous and foolish, and become legally trapped as well.

—An amateur would not have access to vast backup facilities: hospital equipment, medical reference libraries and specialists.

All true, but on the other hand:

—We have all seen parents harass and vex their children.

—Each of us has been frustrated by one or more teachers.

—Military personnel are familiar with enraging humiliations.

—Children at play are often cruel.

—Most family quarrels result from a long series of small foolish incidents.

—Many workers quit good jobs because of disgusting leadership.

—People say and do thousands of things to hurt themselves.

*All is done in ignorance of the emotional consequences.*

Many people in other parts of the world still live in filth. Only a few decades ago Americans learned about sewage disposal, pure-water supplies, refrigerating food, immunization and the need to clean wounds. Now we pass this information on to our children. *They need to know!*

At the turn of this century Red Cross First Aid was considered too dangerous for people to know about. "There are already too many quacks playing doctor!" "A little knowledge is a dangerous thing!" But not so dangerous as fearful stupidity. We have learned prevention: safety rules about knives, guns, swimming, fires, medicines, household poisons, fireworks and many other things. We teach our teenagers what can safely be done on the spot to prevent further suffering: clean wounds, splint broken bones, extract poisons, treat for shock, apply artificial respiration, apply tourniquets. We teach them about emergencies which require prompt medical attention: heart attack, dog bite, appendicitis, unexplained fever, concussion. It is hard to believe that there could have been serious opposition to teaching people Red Cross First Aid.

Why have we waited so long for Emotional First Aid? Is it too dangerous to fool with people's minds? No! The real danger is from ignorance! We fool with people's minds every day, by teasing, scolding, scaring, tormenting, misguiding, teaching, loving, pampering.

Once it was argued that only a doctor should treat a wound, set a broken bone or give a pill. Now we know that these things must often be done where it is impossible to contact a doctor: on a battlefield or a fishing boat; at a summer camp or remote military site; during a severe storm or flood. Instant aid must be provided for snake bite, poisoning, electric shock, broken bones, severe bleeding. Those who resisted the First Aid program visualized the least able, the least informed, playing doctor. Eventually thousands of intelligent citizens, many with college degrees, proved that they could make good use of basic medical supplies and a book of simple instructions.

CHAPTER 2

# *Something Can Be Done*

People have been rendering Emotional First Aid since time began. It is natural to offer sympathy, relieve pain and help in many other ways. Self-help is sometimes more difficult, and perhaps more dangerous, than helping another. This is logical: one characteristic of emotional shock is loss of common sense and reasonable perspective. A person who is spinning is less likely to care for himself and avoid danger than an observer. Getting drunk and committing suicide are common, but hardly successful actions for solving or evading emotional crises.

Something sensible can be done in every emotional crisis or traumatic event. At least one of the following suggestions can be applied on the spot.

## EMOTIONAL FIRST AID PROCEDURES

1. *Buddy system.* When someone is in emotional shock, don't leave him alone; don't let him work, go home or sleep alone. He might suddenly be overwhelmed with a destructive idea. If you are in shock, stay with someone, for hours or days if necessary.

2. *Assume guard position.* This has two parts. (1) This is more formal than being a buddy. For instance, at the scene of an accident or disaster the patient may be unconscious. You might direct traffic, keep him warm, start a written report, send for help. (2) If you too are directly involved and realize that you are experiencing emotional shock, you can retain a measure of composure and self-protection by concentrating on the tasks at hand. You may postpone your own shock symptoms until a more convenient time.

3. *Remedy physical problems.* Furnish food and warmth; furnish medical aid; send for the tow truck; put out the fire; take care of the kids; relieve anxiety by helping.

4. *Direct command.* A direct order or the need to perform

duties tends to dispel confusion and uncertainty. A boss, parent, doctor, lawyer or teacher may properly give advice or a command. Outside "force" seems to help a man hold himself together. If in shock, he may obey as a semi-conscious robot, but that is better than hysteria or slumping into a coma.

5. *Sleep.* For some situations a short nap does the trick, relieves tensions and provides a fresh start. Others may require sleeping twelve hours a day for a week.

6. *Stimulant.* Coffee or a wake-up pill can help the whole world seem brighter and more hopeful. It should help one to make decisions, solve problems and stir oneself to action.

7. *Change environment.* Go somewhere else until you feel better. Get away from the people. Indulge in some fun. Let the problem and its solution wait if possible.

8. *Vigorous exercise.* Do some physical labor; take long walks; get extra fresh air into the lungs; tire the body so it must sleep in spite of nervous tensions.

9. *Ask for help.* It is surprising to learn of the people who suffer in silence. Some are too timid or proud to ask. Some don't know that there are many kinds of social agencies, many offering *free* services.

10. *T.L.C.—Tender Loving Care.* Sympathy, caring, doing a little extra, showing compassion, sincere personal attention, dedicated affectionate consideration.

11. *Listen.* Help him talk it out. If possible, get him to repeat it twenty times. Repetition is surprisingly therapeutic. It may prevent a subconscious hangup (phobia or compulsion).

12. *List facts.* List known factors, and list unknown factors. Describe the situation in great detail. This may dispel fear and confusion and sometimes turns up a clue leading to a solution.

13. *Confront.* Honest discussion; stop running away; bring the matter to a head; take the bull by the horns. "How much of it was *your* fault?" "How important is this matter, after all?" "What is the worst that can happen?" Help him decide on some reasonable self-help course of action.

14. *New data.* Offer new facts that could help him solve his problem. Mention similar cases that had successful conclusions. Suggest choices of action.

## Something Can Be Done

15. *Control environment.* Make something, fix something, do any kind of useful work; eliminate threats, stop noise, haul in some wood; positive action reverses negative conditions and moods. Doing something makes you feel less helpless.

16. *Remedy havingness.* Every emotional shock represents or causes a psychic loss. Replace the losses with small gifts, food, compliments. Buy something. Give something. Some people go out on the town to restore their feeling of well-being.

17. *Grief work.* The death of a loved one causes grief, a compulsion to cry and mourn. To mourn a death is proper and healthful. It is recommended that a certain period be set aside every day to grieve. It may take up to six weeks to cry dry. If this is not done, the grief may be stored in the subconscious and cause trouble for years.

18. *Psychodrama.* Mothers of small children can "kiss it" to make the hurt go away. A little pink pill does wonders for some people, even though it is pure sugar or baking soda. Witch doctors rely on hocus-pokus. Modern psychiatrists sometimes ask their patients to act out an imaginary scene depicting their fears or hostilities.

19. *Vent anger.* Anger creates tremendous psychic energy which must be discharged. Some people sock punching bags, chop wood or hammer nails, while swearing violently. There are funny stories about the "pecking order" at the shop or office: the boss growls at the manager, etc., down the line of lesser employees to the floor sweeper; he has to control himself until he gets home, where he has the right to kick the cat. Kicking stones relieves some people.

20. *Finish the cycle.* Fall off the bike? Don't quit; try again. To quit something that is potentially dangerous in the midst of a painful incident is to risk a hangup. In professional psychotherapy it is sometimes necessary to recall almost-forgotten incidents, even back to childhood, in order to finish some unfinished business artificially, thus clearing a subconscious hangup.

21. *Counter shock.* This is an extreme measure to counter violent hysteria. A gunshot might stop a mob; a slap in the face might calm a frightened woman; a sock on the chin might subdue a drowning man; a spanking might quell a tantrum.

22. *Overwhelming.* Soldiers call this "pulling rank." In legal terms it is a court order. In industry it is "a direct order." This refers to the powerful, last-word, final-authority relationship between parent and child, doctor and patient, professor and student. The temporary therapeutic value is derived by settling an issue clearly and finally. This eliminates bickering, indecision and confusion.

23. *Induction.* Sometimes our emotions tend to harmonize, or tune in, with the emotional tone of people around us. It is easy to be sad at a funeral. In mob rule scores of people are swayed to do foolish things. It is easy to study among serious students. It seems easy to work with other willing workers. Bystanders become upset at an accident; they feel an urge to participate when a fight starts. Conversely, a calm, confident leader can control a nervous group with almost no effort. The group looks to him and finds serenity. A small child scared by a bad dream may get into bed with his parents and find infinite security there. A powerful magnet induces magnetism in other pieces of iron if they are close. Powerful personalities induce responses in people near them.

24. *Communicate.* Problems are caused by *not* communicating or by *mis*communicating. When an emotional problem is identified, *more* communication is required. Tell someone your troubles. Go out on the town or go to church. You may need to seek medical or legal advice. It is natural for a person in emotional shock to tend to stop communicating, especially about his problem. He doesn't want to look at or think about where he really hurts. Finally, years later, his psychiatrist will laboriously search for the hidden hurt and force him to communicate about it.

25. *Medical aid.* Almost any physical illness can cause poor spirits and tiredness. Doctors should be consulted about hormone imbalance, poor diet, defective eyesight. Tranquilizers and energizers can be helpful when used properly. Even placebos (make-believe medicines) can relieve nervousness and anxiety. Dentists and plastic surgeons can make fine contributions to a person's self-image and self-confidence.

26. *Charm schools.* Confidence, social graces and the skills

needed to communicate easily are seldom found in their natural state. They must be learned and cultivated. Teenagers of both sexes need dancing school, public speaking, dramatics classes and music lessons. Such instruction teaches them courtesy and self-control, gives them a sense of belonging. Perhaps most important of all, they learn socially acceptable ways of showing off.

27. *Emergency procedure.* Plan what you should do "in case." This is true prevention, since you can certainly do better planning *before* a traumatic situation spins you into an emotional shock. Some people turn to booze; a few faint. List sources of help: police, fire department, doctor, close relatives, the minister, the boss. Teach your children how to get help, both at home and away from home.

28. *Confession.* (1) Admit your mistake; make amends. This is certainly a step toward emotional maturity! (2) From the religious and/or psychological view, confession *is* good for the soul if your problem involves a sense of moral guilt.

29. *Prayer.* Prayer brings comfort to some, and inspiration. Let's include here reading the Bible and other inspirational material, meditation, religious music and drama.

30. *Stable data.* This means a faith to live by—not necessarily a religious faith but one that is vitally important to some. Others believe in the ultimate power of education, money, democracy or the golden rule. Without stable data all is confusion: nothing matters and no one cares.

31. *Conserve energy.* If you seem to be tired all the time, or it seems that little things keep you so busy or so tired that really important projects suffer, then cut your program. Don't spread yourself too thin. Wouldn't it be better to drop a course or two than to quit college altogether?

32. *Cut down.* Remember the motto about moderation? Your tiredness or irritability may be caused by too much coffee, Coke, tobacco, pills, booze, spices or night life.

33. *Switch roles.* Be your other self for a while. Each of us leads a double life: we play two or more parts, or roles. A college student may be a tiger at his fraternity and Mother's little boy at home.

34. *Music*. Marches, polkas, waltzes, hymns, ballads—music can soothe, or arouse emotions. Singing or playing music calms nerves, raises spirits, changes moods.

35. *Logic*. Contemplating great ideas, inspirational reading, utilizing formulas for problem solving.

36. *Referee*. Some kinds of fights and quarrels can be settled by allowing a third party to act as referee. This is often successful in family counseling. Schoolboys often put on the gloves to settle disputes.

37. *Positive thinking*. "Psycho-cybernetics," "TNT," formerly known as pollyanna-ism. They really work to help people solve problems and feel better.

38. *Validate*. ("To recognize as true and valuable.") This means many wonderful things: to meet with approval, sometimes applause; to be a winner; to be valued highly; to be trusted, admired; to be wanted.

39. *Control*. Systematic action with a purpose; sensible rules; disciplined conscience; governing restraint; regulation. *Good* control is a key principle in achieving emotional maturity and abundant living.

40. *Recall moments of success*. The human spirit derives great pleasure and courage from remembering previous successful experiences. Merely the mention of a few tough problems you solved, a few fights you won, some really good projects you finished—those memory pictures have confidence, enthusiasm and good feeling that splash right into present time. (This is a special type of positive thinking.)

You see! *Something can be done* to avoid or relieve most kinds of everyday emotional problems. (Serious, chronic, dangerous mental illnesses will be discussed in a later chapter.)

These forty suggestions are listed *very* briefly. A class could take each one for a fifty-minute period and explore it in depth, perhaps listing several real-life case histories, referring to published articles on the subject or using the idea as the basis for a sensitivity-development exercise. Students who have a special interest, such as family counseling or scouting, may find themselves checking the points they wish to practice and become specialists in.

CHAPTER 3

# *What Is Emotional Health?*

### NOT HURTING TOO BAD

Mental health clinics are being established in most cities. They are for people who have painful emotional problems, such as a growing fear of self-destruction, inability to find or hold a job, amnesia, unexplained fits of anger or fear, or some strange overpowering obsession. Clinical counselors try to help them to reestablish their former state of emotional equilibrium—that is, help them to stop hurting and return to normal, whatever normal was.

The goals of the clinics are to (1) avoid complete emotional collapse or irreversible crisis; (2) be somebody who cares when nobody else does; (3) relieve or cure the emotional pain; (4) keep people in their own homes, and earning their own living if possible, rather than let them get worse and become wards of the state.

This type of clinical service does not include complete psychological testing or evaluation. Time does not permit psychoanalysis, overcoming personality quirks or reinforcing long-standing emotional weak spots. Charges for service are based on ability to pay. Most problems are solved in six counseling sessions or less.

Compare this definition of emotional health with a used car salesman's meaning of "It's a good car." The ten-year-old car was towed in; it wouldn't run. The mechanic put in new points, charged the battery, washed the car. Now it starts every time and looks good. Restoring an antique auto to mint condition is an entirely different matter.

### SYMPTOMS OF MENTAL ILLNESS

Mental health is the absence of mental illness. Therefore, if you don't have these sick symptoms you must be healthy:

1. Parasitic dependence, unable to be responsible for own daily needs or social life. Unable to make practical decisions.
2. Selfish. Very demanding, seldom giving or sharing.
3. Inferiority complex. Always competing, showing off compulsively, acting like a clown.
4. Poor self-image. Doesn't like own looks, unsatisfied with own achievements, guilty about bad habits, often late.
5. Communication poor. Unwilling and unable to discuss problems, ask for help, write letters, settle business matters.
6. Bad temper. Frequently displays cruelty, hostility and anger; discourteous; destructive.
7. Unrealistic, unreasonable. Calls white black; out of present time—that is, reliving old times, past victories and failures.
8. Nervous. Can't sleep well, has nightmares, tics and twitches.
9. Psychosomatic problems. Physical ailments with no organic causes; may be a hypochondriac.
10. Tired most of the time, lacks interest, unable to have fun, unable to enjoy work.
11. Moody. Changes personality suddenly.
12. Goes into trance. Hears and see things, blacks out.
13. Preoccupied with thoughts of death, murder, suicide, etc.
14. Cannot control his environment. Belongings in chronic disrepair, accident-prone, breaks things, they get lost.
15. Has poor "games." Compulsively spoils things for others; cheats, lies, quits, changes sides, betrays secrets.

## MENTAL HEALTH

Positive, vigorous, dynamic, vital, successful, happy. Mental health is much more than "normal," more than "natural." Mental health comes from intelligent planning, skillful training, determined attention to future goals. Purpose, system, discipline. Emotional maturity does not come with years.

1. Personally responsible. Independent; makes practical plans and sees them through; admits mistakes.
2. Thoughtful, generous, sympathetic.
3. Avoids extreme indulgences; advocates sensible moderation in all things.

# What Is Emotional Health?

4. Good self-image. Modest but self-assured, making steady progress on self-improvement; guards honor and self-respect.

5. Communicates easily and skillfully; seeks or offers help readily as required; shares enthusiasm and philosophy.

6. Adjusts to avoid unnecessary conflict; natural peacemaker; offers encouragement and appreciation.

7. Realistic, analytical, reasonable; judges values on a gradient scale; lives in present time.

8. Good nerves and self-control; relaxes easily, sleeps well.

9. Healthy attractive body. Bright eyes, heals wounds quickly, overcomes infections and poisons promptly.

10. Energetic, ambitious. Enjoys working, willing to do a little extra. Inspires enthusiasm in others.

11. Stable personality. No awkward unexplained moods.

12. High tolerance for disorder, discourtesy and confusion when unavoidable; retains self-control and perspective.

13. Controls environment, utilizes useful habits and purposeful routines, is systematic and orderly. Belongings are kept in good repair, seldom lost or broken; seldom has an accident.

14. Thinks positive. Enjoys talking or reading great ideas, plans fascinating projects; works puzzles and solves problems for the fun of it.

15. Has good "games" and helps others to have good games.

## GRADIENT SCALE

So far we have interesting valid items which should be included in a definition of emotional health, but they don't seem to work right. The clinical definition is in practical use, but only in clinics. One chart is *all* negative, and probably doesn't fit anyone we know. It is sick, sick, sick. The other chart describes a genius or saint, and there isn't much need for *that*. If one chart is all "black," and the other chart is all "white," what we need is a "gray" chart. We can put "terrible" at the bottom, and "perfect" at the top. Everyone can find his shade of gray between the two extremes.

"*Normal.*" Sociologists testing large groups of students and workers find that "normal" is about mid-scale, halfway up. Most of the people we know are "upper normal."

Most of the non-achievers are low-scale.
Most of the champions and lucky people are high-scale.
Low-scale people have more troubles.
High-scale people have more fun.
Low-scale people seldom win (seldom succeed).
High-scale people almost always win.

## STUDY THE GRADIENT SCALE

Read down each column in the chart "Levels of Emotional Maturity" and pick out your level. Mark it. When you have finished all columns, connect each mark with a solid line to make a sort of graph. This is your shade of gray. Use different colors to plot people you know. Such graphs make it possible to report or record large amounts of psychological information systematically, rapidly and impersonally.

Note that there is a general agreement of scores in most of the columns, with only an occasional really high or low mark. A low-scale person tends to be low in all things, and a high-scale person tends to be high in all things. Hence it is possible to estimate a person's attitudes on many subjects by evaluating only a few. Emotional First Aid tries to estimate a person's scale level, then do whatever can be done to improve or raise his level.

Yes, it is certainly possible for people to be high-scale sometimes and low-scale at others. One definition of emotional maturity: high-scale most of the time, but low-scale (in anger, fear, grief or apathy) when appropriate. Emotional sickness is *being stuck* at *any* level.

| | Emotion Being Expressed | Physical Health | Ability to Learn | Reacts with Environment | Versatility | Self-image | Cares | Games vs. Problems | Potential Success |
|---|---|---|---|---|---|---|---|---|---|
| 12 | Eager | Immune No accid. Heal quickly No psycho-somatics | Keen interest Thirst for knowledge | Systematic Confident Control | Very versatile Flexible, Adaptable | Confident Satisfied Mature Dynamic | Strong active interest in many things | Maker of games Trouble-shooter | Certain in all endeavors Excellent |
| 11 | Strong interest | | | | | | | | |
| 10 | | | | | | | | | |
| 9 | Some interest | Seldom sick Few accidents | Good Average | Usually satisfact. control | Changes if necess. Trainable | Modest Content Low confidence Inactive | Some interest Little interest | Plays games Few problems. | Very good Good |
| 8 | | | | | | | | | |
| 7 | Content | | | | | | | | |
| 6 | Bored Indifferent | Normal arthritis ulcers migraine etc. | Interest only in violence. ie: BIG action | Clumsy Sloppy Destructive Unreliable | Resists change Stubborn refusal | Victim Crusader (must defend) | Watches others Physical interests | Pieces in games of others Many problems | Sporadic Occasionally in some areas |
| 5 | Open resentment | | | | | | | | |
| 4 | | | | | | | | | |
| 3 | Anger | accident-prone hazard! | Poor Garbles informat. Can't remember | Tries to adjust Confined in envir. | Hostile fearful submission Stupid | Identity uncertain scapegoat | Danger Animal senses | No game condition Constant problems | Seldom Never |
| 2 | Hostility | | | | | | | | |
| 1 | Fear | | | | | | | | |

CHAPTER 4

# *The Game of Life*

A survey was made (in New Jersey) to determine which class of people was the happiest and had the fewest frustrations. The researchers had hoped to prove that the people with the most education were the happiest. Somewhat dismayed, they found that the skilled blue-collar worker is the most contented. He earns a good wage, usually enjoys his work, has relatively little responsibility to worry about. He lives in comfortable leisure, has opportunities to seek promotions or change jobs. He has a wide variety of entertainment and hobbies. He has good economic security. When he comes home from work, he can kick off his shoes, open a beer and sit down to watch TV.

What is happiness? What is success? What is "abundant living"?

One answer would be: plenty of good food, physical health, a warm home, personal security, a family to love, friends and an interesting job.

A high-class philosophical answer could be: having "good games." We can describe "abundant living" by discussing the elements of a good game. If you are not an athlete and don't play cards, you may resist the idea of considering all of life as a big game. Life is much more serious!

"Game" is used here as a symbol for a philosophical theory or point of view. The game theory helps explain people's peculiar attitudes and actions, and it is a reliable clue for solving some kinds of emotional problems.

## GAME FORMULA

Children, puppies and kittens learn to play games intuitively. They catch on to the fun of chasing a ball or playing hide and seek or wrestling as soon as their little bodies are able. There is

# The Game of Life

no reward for all that effort except the fun of it. Why, then, tear a game into little pieces for study? In this way we will gain the necessary understanding for fixing games that aren't fun and for making wonderful new games.

Two terms are used over and over in Emotional First Aid: "good games" and "no-game condition." They mean, respectively, "having fun and adventure" and "no fun, and hopeless, that is, no chance to win or make things get better." "Having good games" means being happy, and you may learn something new about games every day of your life. This theory is one of the fundamentals of abundant living.

## INGREDIENTS OF A GAME

*Place.* playing field, table, board. You need a chess board to play chess, a ball field to play ball, a pool to swim in. If they go on with their plans to blow up the whole world, that will spoil *all* games.

*Goal.* What is the prize? When does the game end? How can we tell who wins? What is this game really about?

*Opponent.* The enemy; opposition; other player, the odds, resistance to be overcome; work to be done; that which keeps the player from achieving the goal instantly and effortlessly. This may be an unknown factor (mystery), as in solving a puzzle or a crime or in scientific research.

*Rules.* Legal moves, fouls; positions of teammates; point system for scoring; rights and duties of players.

*Risk.* What does the loser lose? There must be a penalty for not winning. What are the stakes? What is the ante? What is the discomfort which must be avoided?

*Challenge.* The real possibility, the threat of losing; a *worthy* opponent with skill and power sufficient to require us to do our best. Caring enough. Playing for keeps.

*Worthy teammates.* Also good umpires, judges, if required.

*Willingness to lose.* Not willing to bet your reputation, all your worldy wealth, your life? Then don't play!

*Sportsmanship.* Know the rules and keep them. Ignoring rules or cheating spoils the game. Insist on fair play, or winning will lose its savor.

*Sense of motion.* A game is a cycle of events; certain things are supposed to happen in such a way that there is pleasure in playing no matter who wins. Events must occur fast enough, but not too fast. Too slow means boredom; too fast means confusion.

*Skill.* Coaching, training, discipline, experience, practice.

*Communication.* Giving and receiving meaningful signals.

*Awareness and ability.* Aliveness and willingness; being in training; being qualified; being in the right league; being prepared.

*Mockups* (mockup: a scale model, not the real thing). It is very important for a person to be able to visualize a past or future condition so clearly that he can enter into the imaginary scene and "try it on." He must be able to recall or forecast the outcome of his actions and clearly sense his personal pleasure or pain. The value of experience is based on recall. Motivation and ingenuity are based on mockups of possible futures.

## GRADIENT SCALE OF GAMES

Games vary in complexity, degrees of risk and interest. Not all games are fun for all people. People should be urged or permitted to choose their own games, upgrading or downgrading as required until they find levels which are personally satisfying and meaningful.

## LEVELS OF GAMES

| | | |
|---|---|---|
| Engineers, Big-Businessmen | Create games | Wide variety |
| Technicians, supervisors | Play games | Some choices |
| Homemakers, laborers | | Limited choices |
| Gamblers, military | | Specialized games |
| Slaves | Pieces in games of others | No game, no choice, meaningless |
| "Warm bodies" | What game? | Nothing matters |

*Career.* Ask parents what they want their children to be when they grow up. Ask teenagers what they are going to be when they graduate; you will get dozens of different good answers. Most parents don't really care whether their son becomes a doctor, teacher or farmer, *so long as he is happy.* They hope his career will be both challenging and satisfying—that he will have good games.

*Infinite security.* Would you like to win a contest which furnished you a fine apartment, food, recreation and all expenses paid for the rest of your life—with one stipulation: you could not leave your apartment? You wouldn't have to try, since you couldn't fail. No competition. You couldn't get hurt. Complete safety; years of boredom.

Few healthy people would willingly give up their chance for adventure and games.

Dr. Eric Berne's book *Games People Play* has many amusing examples of grown-up social games.

It is immoral to spoil someone's game unnecessarily. Ask an athlete what he thinks of someone who tries to play but doesn't know the rules, or who cheats. Ask him what he thinks of a player who doesn't play for keeps, that is, who is halfhearted, unenthusiastic, doesn't care. Any applications here to school, home, church or on the job?

CHAPTER 5

# *Communication Technology*

One of man's basic problems is learning to communicate more effectively. Garbled communications cause a large percentage of emotional problems. Problem *solving* of all kinds presumes that communication will be optimum—that is; that all parties involved will know how and be willing and that all communications will be appropriate, complete and effective. Actually few people can explain what a communication is; they don't know what things can go wrong; they probably don't know for certain whether they got through or not.

Communicating is like driving a car: as long as everything is going okay, why worry about it? Millions of people graduate from school, earn a good living and raise happy families without studying the technical details involved in communicating. But in today's world there are millions of people who are not finishing school, who are not satisfied with their jobs and whose family life is ragged. Everything isn't going okay. If the exact psychological trouble can be found soon enough and repaired, untold years of suffering may be averted. Jail sentences, lifelong unemployment or poverty and divorce may be avoided. To fix a complicated system, whether a car or a human personality, we must take time to learn the theory of operation.

## COMMUNICATION FORMULA/THEORY

*Sender*. Mr. A. The person or station wishing to communicate.

*Receiver*. Mr. B. The person for whom the communication is intended.

*Particle*. The message or object which is being sent.

*Mass of particle*. The size, weight, bulk or importance. A box of fine chocolates has a different "mass" than a single jelly bean. A 30-30 rifle bullet has a different "mass" than a 22.

*Velocity.* The physical speed of the particle. Usually, the greater the velocity, the more effective the communication. Air mail is better than a regular first-class letter; a telegram is better than air mail; and a telephone call is far nicer than a telegram.

*Space.* The distance between A and B. Communication becomes more difficult as distance increases.

*Intention of the sender.* This refers to the care and determination of Mr. A. (sender) to make his message effective and completely understood. The sender should be precise and deliberate.

*Attention of receiver.* Is he turned on, tuned in and listening/watching? Is he watching TV instead of paying heed to your message?

*Ability of the receiver to duplicate* (receive). Is his radio, TV or teletype machine turned on? If the message is in code, can Mr. B decode it? If Mr. A is sending food, is it a kind that Mr. B likes to eat? If Mr. A is sending a letter in German, can Mr. B read German?

*Acknowledgment.* Mr. B must acknowledge receipt of the communication to Mr. A to complete the cycle. The sooner the better, too. People get very nervous, and sometimes angry, if their efforts to communicate are ignored. Usually, if Mr. A does not get an acknowledgment promptly, he will start again. Sometimes when Mr. A fails to receive an acknowledgment two or three times, he will conclude that Mr. B doesn't care; then Mr. A stops trying to send. All communication may become blocked when Mr. B fails to reply, "Okay, I got it."

*Many things can happen to a communication to degrade it. A troubleshooter (or psychotherapist) should be familiar with these possibilities. These terms are obviously taken from the electronic industry, but the principles apply in everyday life.*

*Distortion.* The particle gets changed between A and B. Something may be added, or taken away. Some of the eggs may get broken. The flowers may wilt. Part of a letter might be censored. A picture might have some trick photography.

*Interference.* Noise, static, a baby crying in church, the evening paper soaked with rain, mosquitos at a beach party.

*Attenuation.* The signal gets weaker and weaker. The ice melts before the picnic; some of the pay check gets spent before you even get it home; enthusiasm and encouragement can be attenuated by delaying a response.

*Metacom. Meta* = before, after, above, below, among, between, around; *com* = communication.

A metacom is a communication which is superimposed on another communication. It is what is read between the lines. It may be part of a figurative expression not to be taken literally. It is an inference, an implication. It might be the meaning in a special tone of voice or the use of certain symbols.

Metacoms are secret messages. Often they are coded, and if you don't know the code you miss the meaning. Cliques and "in" groups have their own little winks and knowing smiles. Children and adults who are used to working and playing together seem to know intuitively; they tune in on bits of messages that fly back and forth. Newcomers know they shouldn't take too much for granted at first, until they become familiar with the metacom codes.

We have common expressions which refer to the metacom:
"Double talk."
"He knows I'm only kidding."
"What you do speaks louder than what you say."
"Snow job" means, "I heard what you said, but I don't believe it."
"I hear you saying . . ." is often used in counseling sessions to reflect back to the patient some unreasonable remark so that he can hear how it sounds.

Little children (and animals) must rely on metacom almost entirely. They are born with ESP, and manage to tune in without knowing the meaning of words. They learn easy messages like "I like you," "You can trust me to hold you" and "I am going away."

Metacoms cause problems in family life, on the job, at school and in religion. People are usually unaware that they are sending or receiving metacoms. Yet the metacom is the really important part of the message. It is the *real* truth no matter what your words seem to say.

Two people living or working in the same area, such as spouses, cannot *not* communicate. Even silence says something!

Schizophrenia is caused by long exposure to double meaning, double bind, double level of emotions. The ultimate dilemma: "Which is which and what is what? Is there anything I can be sure of? Does anything really matter? Who cares?"

*Hum.* The little soft sounds radios make because they are plugged into the power line. Hum spoils soft violin or flute solos. Hum is a little background disturbance, usually unnoticed, but sometimes an annoying nuisance. Hum is like counting votes at a convention. Hum is a little like having big sister quietly busy within earshot when you want to have a man-to-man talk with a 13-year-old son.

*Rattle.* Noise of loose or broken parts. A loud-speaker that rattles spoils the music. A rattle in a car signals real trouble. So do clanks, squeaks and crunches. With people, this equates with teasing, bullying, smashing dishes, slamming doors. Harsh, abrupt, inappropriate, uncontrolled, distracting.

*Fading.* Unreliable, sometimes entirely non-existent when required; short-wave overseas radio broadcast; local radio at night.

*Limiting.* Compression, de-emphasis of major signals. This is like going to a restaurant and eating so much soup and salad that you have to get a doggie bag for most of your steak and you don't have room for dessert.

*Expansion.* Exaggerating, causing small things to seem large.

*Attenuation.* Signal gets weaker and weaker (never fades back in). This is what happens to communications when friends move away. Letters get fewer and shorter and finally stop.

*Narrow band.* Tunnel vision, half-truth, abbreviated. A summary of a story. An outline of a speech. "Broad band" means getting everything, even smallest details. In TV a narrow-band receiver shows harsh black and white, with almost no gray tones; a broad-band system is required to show fine color.

*Filter.* To take out or remove some particular item or portion and let the rest go through. Filtering may remove unwanted distractions; it may tend to strain out and purify. On the other hand, it may filter out and remove important ingredients. Parents tend to filter out remarks about sex from their conversation when children are present; thin walls in apartment houses tend to filter out the high notes from the neighbor's hi-fi, so you hear mostly boom-boom bass.

*Cross-talk.* Two or more signals mixed; hearing strange voices on the telephone while you are talking to a friend; two people trying to talk at once at a meeting.

*Garble.* So much error that the received fragments are useless; in teletype, a continuous string of letters and spaces which don't spell words or make any sense; a baby jabbering; some of the instruction sheets published by government agencies.

*Harmonic distortion.* Additional tones sneak in between A and B, in multiples of the fundamental tones. We end up with more tones than we started with; therefore the reproduction/duplication cannot be true and pure. With people, Mr. B would say, "But I thought you meant . . . ," and Mr. A would say, "But that isn't what I said!"

*Impedance mismatch.* Wrong speed or voltage or pressure. This is like trying to start driving a car in high gear or driving on the open highway in low gear. It is like plugging your 110-volt electric razor into your 12-volt car system. With people it is like inviting your local minister to a stag party or expecting your husband to understand why the colors in the wallpaper have to match colors in the rug, sofa and drapes.

*Poor indexing.* Referring to an automatic record player, this means that the tone arm drops in the middle of the first tune. On a tape recorder it means that when you try to speed in to hear a selection in the middle of the tape, the tape snarls when you stop. The same with people: they may start too soon or not soon enough; they may not know where to start or when to stop; they lose things and can't remember. Some always arrive late.

*Ghost.* In TV it means phase distortion, echo, reflection, double image. Schizophrenic? Putting on airs; hinting; alluding; casting aspersions; making believe.

*Out of sync.* Synchronization is critical in TV, teletype, wirephoto and FM stereo. The bits of message sent from A must be reassembled in exactly the right order at B. A sync signal is

# Communication Technology

sent simultaneously with the message bits; if the sync signal is lost, the picture or telegram or stereo music cannot be *duplicated* at the receiver.

With people it is being exactly together when singing a duet; gracefulness when dancing; being in step when marching. Some things people do must be locked-in-sync to go smoothly, otherwise clumsiness, confusion and frustration will result.

*Reversal.* A photographic negative is reversed: the sky looks black; a black cat looks white. A reflection in a mirror shows lettering backward. The ground glass in the back of a big camera shows things upside down.

*Multiplex.* To send several messages by the same route at one time. FM stereo transmits the left and the right audio channels on the same radio beam. TV stations send both picture and sound on the same radio beam. People talk with their mouths, eyes, shaking their heads and waving their hands all at once. They are also sending "metacom."

*Format.* The layout of formal communications; the usual sequence; the style; a typical program or service, such as for a musical concert or church service. Industries have standard employment applications. A format helps keep continuity throughout a series of ads, booklets, catalogues or reports. The format makes it easier to prepare a communication because there is a place for each item; important items cannot be forgotten; no time is required to arrange the material each time; it is easier to locate specific information if it is listed in its proper place.

*Outline.* An outline is a scaffold on which to build written reports and stories. It can be the framework for a speech.

*Vocabulary.* Words, symbols, special technical theories, formulas for discussing, or even thinking about, scientific material and other specialized subjects, such as art, music and cooking.

*Terminals.* Mr. A and Mr. B are terminals. A bus station and an airport are terminals. Communications start and stop at terminals. In the usual sense "terminal" means at the end. There is another meaning: a terminal is where connections are made. For instance, an employment agency connects employers with employees; a public dance helps people to meet other people.

*Code.* (1) Morse code is an example of systems for converting words and numbers into pulses or tones (dots and dashes) which can be transmitted more easily and more economically. For instance, messages can be sent several miles using a flashing light. (2) A system of rules and regulations, such as a building code or a code of conduct. Codes speed communication.

*Delay.* To move too slowly, put off till a future time, procrastinate, postpone, retard, temporarily stop.

*Feedback.* "The transfer of information or energy from the output of a circuit or system back to the input." Positive feedback reinforces the original input signal; it is called regeneration. Negative feedback (degeneration) opposes the original signal. Both are useful in electronics, mechanics and human affairs. When a bride receives praise for her attempts at cooking, this positive feedback will make her want to cook more. Scolding a child for spraying water all over the kitchen will decrease his desire to do that (negative feedback).

*Speed.* (Not velocity, mentioned earlier.) Rapidity of motion or action; rate of performance; ratio of work done to time spent. Some people talk too fast. A phonograph or tape recorder must be set at the right speed. Skill in athletics depends on fast reaction time. Students read at different speeds; one may read two books while his friend reads one. Modern computers perform simple functions in a millionth of a millionth of a second (picosecond).

*Repetition.* Making, doing or saying something again. Repeating is an expensive waste of time but is sometimes necessary, when the first attempt is unsuccessful. On the other hand, repetition helps us to learn. It is practice and experience.

*Pictures.* "One picture is worth ten thousand words." If we include sign language, demonstrations and mimicry, we have the simplest, oldest, most natural scheme for communication.

## PRACTICAL APPLICATIONS

If it is true that all political, social and personal problems are caused by poor communication, then learning new communication skills will be a powerful problem-solving tool. It is sug-

## Communication Technology

gested that those interested in specialized emotional problems, such as those listed on page 12, should make a list of typical case problems, then analyze the communication hangups involved. Finally, practical solutions can be recommended.

Attention is especially directed to the hard-core tough nuts. These are real opportunities for proving that communication is the common denominator in problem solving and a basis for emotional maturity.

Study groups will be able to share dozens of typical case histories, anecdotes and personal insights. Many of them will be suitable for publishing in future editions of this book and in specialized workbooks. Please be alert for possible contributions and send them to the publisher. In this way we may accumulate an encyclopedia of vital ideas to pass on to the next generation.

CHAPTER 6

# Care and Feeding of the Body

Physical health is inseparable from mental health. They go up and down together. *Many people do not realize this!* They risk their health—*and a portion of their sanity*—in many foolish ways: excessive smoking, drinking, careless driving, high-risk sports, using dangerous drugs, ignoring the possibility of venereal disease, indulging in dangerous horseplay.

A keen mind is precious. Every physical pain causes some degree of loss of mental ability and creates an emotional scar. Many emotional wounds do not heal but cause suffering for a lifetime. Psychoanalysis case records prove this. Many physical wounds seem to heal, but some leave ugly scars. Broken bones knit together and become usable but become easily fatigued. Joints once broken may ache or become sore and swollen intermittently *for the rest of a lifetime*. One's happiness and sense of well-being are forever tainted by scars and pains. One's confidence and ambition are drastically reduced by stiffness and tiredness.

Much of this suffering can be prevented in two ways. (1) Safety. Don't take unnecessary risks. (2) Prompt, intelligent emotional care after an accident.

## RED CROSS (PHYSICAL) FIRST AID

The Red Cross *First Aid* textbook is excellent. It is *everyone's* business to understand everyday physical dangers and how to avoid them. Everyone needs to know how to take care of himself if injured and what sensible things can be done to help another.

## NUTRITION

Good nutrition is more than not being hungry. Many people even today are not familiar with the principles of and need for a balanced diet. Food poisoning from spoilage in hot weather is

## Care and Feeding of the Body

always possible. Bad water and milk are still possible in rural areas. People should be informed about the unwise use of garden chemicals and household poisons, such as insect sprays, which can get into food. Remember, any illness has emotional problems too.

## ENVIRONMENT

In the natural environment there are many things which can cause nervousness, fear, tiredness and physical illness.
—Excessive heat or cold.
—Lack of oxygen, from excessive altitude for instance.
—Unusual motion: roller coaster, rocking boat in a storm.
—Intense light: sun on snow, arc welding.
—Loud noise: thunder, large firecrackers, guns.
—Noxious odors: putrefied meat, sulphur dioxide, rotten eggs.
—Animals: insects, bats, sharks, snakes, rats.
—Excessive noise: continuous rumble of machinery, continuous high-volume music, airplanes near an airport, an all-night party upstairs, too frequent fire sirens, motor bikes, barking dogs, pounding steam radiators, doors slamming.
—Nothingness: excessive simplicity, solitary confinement.
—Presence of death: at a funeral or disaster area.
Specialized human environments can cause emotional upset:
—Growing up in a slum ghetto: acclimated to poverty and hopelessness.
—Stage fright.
—Mass hysteria.
—Anticipation of doom or disaster: going to dentist, being stopped by a traffic patrolman, prospect of being overwhelmed.
—Becoming lost.

What is the use of listing environmental factors? This is how we learn to recognize them. We should control the environment if possible. If not, we should avoid dangerous situations. If we can neither control nor avoid, at least we can recognize a situation for what it is, look for undesirable emotional effects and proceed with Emotional First Aid.

## DRUGS, GOOD AND BAD

There are safe, useful drugs that everyone should know about and that should be found in First Aid kits and home medicine cabinets. The list includes aspirin and similar preparations, Vicks Vaporub and similar salves, alcohol and other antiseptic solutions for cleansing cuts, quinine for fever, Vaseline, talcum powder. There are many good texts on home remedies.

Pep pills, especially those based on caffeine, and some types of tranquilizers are reasonably safe and useful when used wisely. High-powered prescriptions and narcotics are another matter. Even when they are given under doctor's orders, two problems may exist: taking an accidental or on-purpose overdose; and innocently mixing different kinds of medicines, or a medicine with booze. It has been reported that taking aspirin with certain kinds of soft drink can cause emotional disturbances. Some kinds of medicine are known to have side effects and aftereffects even when taken according to the doctor's direction. It is a reasonable assumption that whenever someone takes medicine, his mental alertness may be somewhat altered, usually impaired.

There are several really dangerous drugs. Most of them cause weird sensations and hallucinations. Some are habit-forming.

## MEDICAL CONDITIONS

There are medical reasons for people having terrible dispositions, being too tired, having body odors, being nervous, skinny or too fat. It is astonishing that some people suffer for months or years with problems that could be solved quickly and at modest cost at a medical clinic.

Items to become familiar with that may affect emotional well-being: infection, hormone imbalance, need for vitamin supplement, eye trouble, bad teeth, sore feet. Sometimes a dental plate, a bit of plastic surgery, a hearing aid, can make wonderful changes in a person's life.

The proper care of expectant mothers is vitally important to the emotional health of the child.

## HEREDITY, FAMILY CUSTOMS, HYGIENE

Some emotional and personality traits are inherited from parents via genes and chromosomes. The theory and control of these matters are outside the subject of First Aid. Family customs are also inherited, or at least passed on by parents to children. Some of these are quite harmful but could be corrected. For example:

—Disdain for "book learning."

—Traditional diet badly out of balance regarding minerals, vitamins, protein, calcium, fresh fruits, etc.

—Poor hygiene training regarding bathing, caring for hair, clothes, dental care.

—Vulgar sex attitudes, or perhaps prudery.

—Immature examples in the use of alcohol, temper tantrums, extreme religious attitudes, poor financial judgment, etc.

—Lack of discipline, self-respect, good manners, etc.

## SEX INFORMATION AND ATTITUDES

School, churches and governments have opinions on these matters, and there are many articles and textbooks worth reading. A brief mention of some of the dilemmas will serve to mark a place in this list of factors affecting human emotions and serve as a starting point for class discussions.

—Nature commands all life forms to seek mates and reproduce. Humans have customs and mores regulating or forbidding the free exercise of human mating instincts. The urge is strong —but wrong.

—Is it better to be well informed on sexual matters and enjoy a certain amount of personal freedom and responsibility, or to remain ignorant (innocent) except for immature guesses and bits of vulgar expressions? One attitude is that the ignorant child will be afraid to try anything and will thus avoid trouble.

—One traditional custom is to preach that sexual thoughts or feelings are wicked and sinful under all conditions. This serves to keep sex underground in polite society but causes guilt complexes and many other weird attitudes that are harmful to adult living.

—Should sex be taught in school, at home or in the back seats of cars? Isn't it true that very few parents even attempt to discuss sex with their children? Shouldn't schools furnish practical, authoritative information that every young person needs to know? We combat the dangers of guns, matches, cars and swimming with good information and careful training: is sex less important?

—Venereal disease and unwed motherhood are on the increase. They cause untold suffering. Can we rely on the "nice" people to reverse the trend? When are they going to do it!

## OBESITY

The following is a thinking exercise which has helped some fat people who gave up on diets and exercises. The facts *seem* logical, and the conversion figures come directly from engineering manuals.

"Your problem isn't that you eat too much, it's that you don't defecate enough! Look at me. I eat all I want of anything I want, but I don't get fat. My body doesn't save food, or calories it doesn't need. It uses what it needs and throws the rest away. Now I will prove to you that the kind and quantity of food you eat have very little to do with your overweight problem."

You can't possibly eat enough food to supply your daily needs in heat and energy. Your body doesn't even pretend to use food for fuel! You have been taught a principle that isn't true, and a theory that doesn't work!

Your body radiates about 2,400 watt-hours in a 24-hour period. This is about 2,064,000 calories. This figure was arrived at by studying an air-conditioning engineering manual. When figuring what size of equipment to order to cool a large office, they estimate that each person gives off as much heat as a 100-watt bulb. A watt-hour is a unit of power which creates about 860 calories. Just sitting there in your office, you can give off more than 8,000 calories per hour every hour. This is really a

## Care and Feeding of the Body

conservative estimate: you can radiate much more if you work outdoors on a cool day where the temperature is, say, 40° instead of 72°.

When estimating how much good rural electrification does farmers, engineers determined that a hired man can pump water or saw wood at about the same rate as a ⅛-horsepower electric motor. Thus in 8 hours he would be able to do about 1 hp. of work. In the other 8 hours of wakefulness he might do half as much "work" while washing his car, mowing the lawn and playing with his kids. (1½ hp. of work). This is about 1½ KWH, or about 1,300,000 calories.

We know the human body has internal losses. It pumps blood (7 tons a day), pumps air to breathe, digests food, etc. Make a generous estimate that it is 50 percent efficient. No matter, the internal power requirements, whatever they are, are converted to heat in the body. This has already been accounted for.

Therefore, we have estimated that a working man would expend more than 2,000,000 calories in heat, and perhaps about 1,300,000 calories in actual work—over 3,000,000 calories!

Three questions are asked: How does 1½ HPH = 1½ KWH? An electrical horsepower is 746 watts. Answer: fractional horsepower motors are not 100 percent efficient. Internal motor losses consume the extra power: hysteresis and copper losses, and bearing friction.

Second question: Are these the same kind of calories used in rating food? Isn't there a thing called "kilo-calorie"? Yes, all of the calculations are in single, or small calories. The kilocalorie (1,000 calories) was formerly used by engineers when discussing the fuel requirements for large boilers in power plants. One B.T.U. equals about 4 kilo-calories.

Third question: We know the body requires oxygen to live, and that it gives off carbon dioxide, a product of oxidation or burning. Doesn't this prove that food is used for fuel, and the answer is simply that the body is very efficient? Carbon dioxide is indeed produced by the human body, in small amounts, but the body does not even try to be efficient! In fact, it wastes most of its food-fuel. All adult animals defecate almost as many pounds of waste per day as they eat.

When a sample of food is placed in a laboratory calorimeter it is burned to an ash; all organic matter is burned, leaving only a small quantity of unburnable minerals. But feces, when dried, burn fine. In fact, in rural areas where there are no trees for fuel, people collect cow dung to cook with. Barnyard manure is highly valued by gardeners for its organic content.

I suppose a scientist could dry human dung so that it could be tested in a calorimeter in order to learn how many calories a person throws away each day. Shouldn't that number be subtracted from the food calories he eats?

Wait, there is an easier way to get rid of unwanted calories and count them as they go. A calorie is the amount of heat required to raise the temperature of 1 gram of water 1 degree centigrade. There are about 453 grams in a pint. There are 36.5 degrees centigrade between ice and body temperature (32°F–98°F). Multiply grams by degrees = 16,535 calories! Drink a pint of ice-cold soft drink and lose 16,000 calories! Even more if you eat the ice.

If these figures don't lie, why do we have to eat to keep strong, and where does our energy come from? Could it be that the body needs food for "spare parts"? We know that babies need food for building bones and muscles—that is, for building blocks. Maybe living things use some kind of psychic energy, a life force.

If calories don't regulate a person's weight, what does? How explain that some people do succeed in losing weight by means of dieting? It would seem that there is an animal instinct, a sort of subconscious pattern, which "programs" our physical appearance.

A few people have been successful in reducing by simply "talking" to their bodies. Hypnosis has helped some. Disciplining oneself to stick to a diet is one way to suggest to the body to lose weight. Exercises are always effective in toning up muscles, im-

## Care and Feeding of the Body

proving circulation and proving to the subconscious that you really do care.

On the theory that a fat body seems to be saving nourishment for fear of hard times ahead, reducing one's meals to a painful minimum would seem to verify its fears. Wouldn't it be sensible to eat more, even filling up on non-fattening foods and wasting some? Tell your body there is lots of food, and more where that came from. Tell it to use what it needs and *throw the rest away*. One way to waste food is to leave a little on your plate. Leave a little milk in your glass. One way to talk to your body: several times a day stand straight and tall, pull in your tummy with both hands and say, "That's the way we want to look."

Bodies do what they think they should, according to some psychic pattern. Case histories reporting successful psychoanalysis prove this. Bodies will keep on doing what they are doing until we find a way to change their little minds.

## CHAPTER 7

# *Havingness*

*Have* = own, possess, be, feel, experience; *ing* = act or art of doing; *ness* = state of being. Havingness, like wetness, darkness, and so on, refers to a relative state of being. It refers to an inner, personal, psychic sense of well-being and security. Havingness is:

—An arbitrary level of well-being; everyone senses his own.
—A ratio between losses and gains in everyday life.
—A state of emotional equilibrium.
—A scheme for referring to psychic energy levels and survival potential; psychic voltage.
—A new word for morale; good havingness causes good morale.
—Emotional reserve. A loss of havingness lowers emotional reserve, lowers a person on the gradient scale of emotions.
—Life force, drive, creativity, aliveness.
—A sense of personal worth and freedom.
—Spirit: a severe loss of havingness results in a broken spirit, good havingness is being in good spirits.
—To have, or to have-not; being lucky, or unlucky.

Possession is a vital psychological concept. We like to get things and approval of others, and we hate to lose things or be criticized. Sudden heavy losses, or continuous small losses, can warp one's personality and outlook on life. Losing money, wrecking a car, losing a job, failing a test or getting injured always causes consternation and a loss of emotional security.

Losses are cumulative in the subconscious mind. The more we lose, the more likely we are to lose. Continuous loss spoils the game, whether it is cards, baseball or the game of life. The steady loser finally takes the attitude, "I can't hope to win, so why try!" Instead of quitting altogether, the loser may attempt to play lesser games far below his real ability, thus wasting his talents. Conversely, as one begins to succeed, it becomes easier to achieve

## Havingness

successfully. If he approaches 100 percent perfection, he will start searching for greater challenges—pro leagues, advanced courses, higher mountains to climb.

The subconscious monitors its control over energy, possessions, games conditions and communication facilities. Each person has a normal supply level of these, to be used and replenished in everyday living. Loss of havingness occurs when our supply level drops too suddenly.

There are common "automatic" psychological losses which are a part of normal everyday living, such as:

—Physical exertion, loss of energy, tiredness.
—Hunger, thirst, malnutrition.
—Exposure to severe weather; getting cold, hot, wet.
—Excessive talking or writing, such as teaching, office work.
—Pain, physical or mental.
—Confusion, uncertainty, fear.
—Negative emotions: boredom, frustration, worry, grief, anger.
—Losing things, either accidentally or by having them taken away.
—Being affected: having things done to you, being teased or picked on, being compelled without choice, excessive motion.
—Sudden loud noises, such as crashes or explosions.
—Continuous high-level ambient noise, rumbles, racket.
—Sudden frightening flashes of brilliant light: photo-flash guns, lightning, nearby explosion.

A few small losses are restored normally. Many small drops cannot be restored fast enough, and we have the last-straw effect. A sudden large overwhelming loss seems to blow a fuse, causing hysteria and emotional shock.

Emotional shock results from overdrawing on the emotional reserve. This is like writing checks without enough money in your bank account. It's like losing flying speed in an airplane. Pilots know that if you stall out, you will stop flying; your plane will just drop out of control. A sudden loss of havingness may cause people to stall out and lose control. Some people faint, some have a tantrum, go into a rage or tears; some have amnesia, and a few commit suicide. A loss of havingness always reduces a person's judgment, good humor, ambition, creativeness and moral responsibility. Just as a plane, to resume normal flying, must regain flying speed, so a person must recover his havingness if he is to resume his normal living.

*Restoring havingness.* Fortunately there are also "automatic" gains in normal everyday living:

—Resting, complete relaxation, sleep.
—Eating, drinking.
—Finishing things, completing cycles, getting caught up.
—Getting things: gifts, purchases (new hats), finding things.
—Singing, playing fun games.
—Discovering, learning, establishing certainty.
—Good control: knowing what you must do, having routines.
—Pleasant communications, getting mail, having a party.
—Getting a compliment; any kind of success, admiration.
—Creating or fixing something, arts and crafts.
—T.L.C.—Tender Loving Care.

To remedy havingness is to take an action to restore psychic well-being, self-confidence, morale, etc.

*High morale* (one definition of good havingness) is a mood and spirit conducive to willing and dependable performance; steady self-control; courageous, determined conduct despite danger and privations; conviction of being in the right and on the way to success; faith in the cause or program, and in the leadership. It is confident, aggressive, resolute, often buoyant spirit of wholehearted cooperation in common effort, often attended by zeal, self-sacrifice. It is indomitable, unconquerable, invincible.

A basic concept is that a loss of havingness can bring on an emotional problem; the problem cannot be solved until havingness has been restored. These are symptoms of emotional shock/low havingness. One or more symptoms may be treated and apparently cured, but until havingness is restored, until the real problem is remedied, more symptoms will appear. Saying this another way, being low on the gradient scale is a problem; there may be a thousand ways to act low-scale; the solution of avoiding low-scale actions is to re-establish high-scale attitudes and conditions. High-scale people either avoid problems or solve them themselves.

## CHAPTER 8

# *Invalidation*

*Invalidate*: To void, make helpless, sick, unimportant; to disqualify, denounce, reject, disown, throw out, ignore, overwhelm.

Invalidation is a behavioral pattern that destroys havingness. It is the most common cause of unnecessary emotional damage and suffering. Much invalidation could be prevented by teaching the principles involved and by improved social training.

How often mothers tell a child he is not wanted, he is clumsy, dumb, ugly or stupid (kidding, of course)! Repeated often enough, and reinforced with pain, such meanness can cause the child to become a hopeless emotional cripple.

Most people do things to hurt themselves; it seems to be part of human nature. Even when we know about this and can watch ourselves doing things we shouldn't, it is almost impossible to stop! Having an "inferiority complex" means that you don't like yourself, and you keep doing things that you don't like and that offend others. You put yourself down. Even if you have a misshapen face or a crippled body, you could learn to be a charming, lovable, vitally useful person. Many a person has succeeded in having his personality and inner self retrained for successful living. This is what psychotherapy is about.

It is easy for a winner to win. He gets renewed enthusiasm and intense interest from success. He can afford to play it bold. So what if he does lose? He has plenty, and there is more where that came from.

Not so for the loser. Slipping down scale on the emotional chart, he first begins to be *careful*. Continuing to lose, he has to pull in his horns to utmost conservatism and practical frugality. As he loses all hope of winning, interest dwindles to *boredom*. Teamwork vanishes and is replaced by suspicion, antagonism, then *anger*. Suppressing anger, he becomes quiet, non-communicative, brooding. By now nothing seems to go right. He fumbles and misjudges; he is "shook" and becomes frantic. Control is gone. He is in emotional shock. Sensing his helplessness, he becomes *afraid*. Failing compulsively now, he even commits sabotage, subconsciously trying to fail. This is *covert hostility,* a devious attempt to retain some measure of initiative and control, even if it is to cause unnecessary trouble for former friends and allies. Realizing his great losses and hopelessness, he displays great *grief*. Attempts at formerly successful life patterns become so confusing and unwieldy that he is forced to give up and drop out. He stops participating, stops trying to play any version of the game. He even stops being a piece in the game. Dropping into *apathy*, he stops trying to solve problems; he doesn't care who loses, or how much. He has become a "warm body," a vegetable.

Marriage partners who invalidate each other slip down-scale from eager creation of a fine home, to become wary, bored, hostile, angry, fearful. Compulsive destruction and sabotage result, followed by grief and finally the hopeless, senseless apathy of waiting for the final divorce decree.

A similar pattern can be observed in school dropouts, military deserters, job quitters and criminals.

Every day someone you know is inflicting an invalidating loss on another human being—*unknowingly*. He may call it kidding or poking fun. It may be in the form of amusing gossip, calling names, ridiculing appearances, finding fault with work, contradicting, interrupting, being rude, winning an argument by outshouting or pulling rank, ignoring attempts at friendship, forgetting to answer, demanding unreasonable performance, growling orders in an unnecessarily gruff manner. Any discourtesy can count as a loss. This is a vital natural law, but violations are so common that we seldom notice.

All the little things add up. An unwarranted criticism, a gruff command, a special courtesy gone unnoticed—these are not reasons for quitting a job or getting a divorce. But the human subconscious enters each one in a little black book. They seem to become part of a permanent record. Just as with the Green Stamps we get at the grocery store: each one has almost no cash value,

# Invalidation

but when the last stamp is pasted in at the bottom of the last page, then all the little stamps accumulated down through the months suddenly become meaningful.

Preventing emotional problems can start with cutting down the frequency of the little things, avoiding unnecessary irritations. Courtesy is vital to emotional health.

## BROWNIE POINTS

Here is a little fable that helps teach the principles of validation and havingness to children.

As every child knows from fairy tales, there are many kinds of angels, gnomes, dwarfs, witches and other lovely or weird people in make-believe land. Take the brownies, now. Their job, or assignment, is to do whatever they can to help people live together peacefully and happily. In the beginning the leader of the brownies called them all together in a meeting and explained everything. One of the rules was—and still is—"It is okay to help people with magic, but be careful that you don't use too much." All was quiet for a moment; then one little brownie raised his hand and asked; "But, sir, how can we tell how much magic to use, and how much is too much?"

The wise brownie chief thought for a moment. "Aha," he said, "people will have to pay for our magic. They can have only as much as they earn, or deserve. We will open a brownie credit account for every person. Every human being will get ten free brownie points to start with. From then on he can earn more, or spend some, or even go broke." That was how the brownie point system was set up.

Brownie points are something like dollars, but of course they are invisible, being make-believe. Here is how they work and what they are good for: A brownie point is good for one small favor from another person. A big favor may cost several points. Everybody knows that you can do several little favors for a stranger because *everybody* starts out with at least ten points. On the other hand, a mean little thing that somebody does *costs* him a brownie point. If somebody starts doing a lot of mean things, he may soon use up all his brownie points, in which case nobody would want to do him a favor at all. He'd just be a mean old cuss, and he'd have to start doing some nice things for people to get the magic of friendship and love back again.

It is important for you to understand the magic part of brownie points. Think of someone who likes to be good. He is always helpful and courteous, neat, prompt, a good sport, gentle with little kids. He earns so many brownie points that everybody wants to do nice things for him. If he accidentally gets into trouble, people try to help him.

They want to believe his explanation. He can borrow money just by asking for it. It is easy for him to get a job. If he did something terrible, people would forgive him and still be friends.

It's like that with grownups too. Friendly folks who like to share things, and help wherever they can, collect a wealth of brownie points. Sometimes they can ask for a job that doesn't exist and get it. With enough brownie points you can borrow a special machine that isn't for sale or rent. You might have a person do you a special favor for free, something so special that you couldn't get it done with real money.

When people say, "The best things in life are free," they mean that some of the nicest things can't be bought with dollars. You can buy them only with brownie points.

\* \* \*

Assuming for the moment that life is a game (see chap. 4), then invalidation is telling a person that he can't play or that he isn't playing right or that he is too small or dumb to play. In a mystical sense, to invalidate a person is to tell him, "You don't belong here. You don't deserve to live. You have no rights. You're not wanted. Go away and disappear. Hide somewhere and wait forever!"

Millions of people have dropped out of normal life. They are now hidden in institutions, truly unwanted, unloved and hopeless. Millions of others are living in the dingy gray lower areas of the emotional scale characterized by hostility, fear and grief.

## Invalidation

There are several distinctive modes of invalidation in common everyday use:

*Overwhelming.* Schoolyard bullies proclaim, "I can tease you and hurt you whenever I please because I am bigger than you, and you can't stop me." Parents tell children, "Don't argue; just do it." Judges tell divorcing husbands, "It really doesn't matter what you say, or whether you are really guilty; you have got to pay." Officers tell enlisted men, "That's an order!"

*Confusion.* Excessive complexity, too much noise, excessive motion, double talk, legal and medical jargon. Confusion means being lost, not certain, insecure, lacking control, not knowing, not winning. Confusion causes a big loss in havingness. Some people delight in confusing others; it's a sort of sport for them.

*Overprotection.* Usually of women or children. People should be allowed some dangers and some losses, otherwise they can't have meaningful games. Saying it another way, people who can't risk losing if they wish are unable to learn values, make decisions, solve problems and assume responsibilities.

*Overpermissiveness* is letting people do anything and everything they can think of, in the name of freedom and self-expression, even though it is dangerous, obscene, immoral or illegal. We have been training hippies at home since they were babies! Secretly we have been instilling into them, "You are not playing the game of life for keeps. Society has stacked the customs and laws so that you can't accept them at face value. Our present-day grown-up games are mostly make-believe. We love you and will always see that you have food and lodging of some sort (you can't lose). It doesn't much matter what you do, but please run outside (somewhere else) to play."

Whatever the old-time religion did or didn't do, it helped people feel that rules for living were important and that someone was keeping score.

*"All men are created equal."* Parents, teachers and political revolutionaries teach this preposterous idea. Whereas the gradient-scale system for evaluating people is sensible and self-evident, the "all are equal" theory invalidates the gradient scale. Real trouble

comes when children figure out that they have been duped by parents and teachers. Either the teachers were mistaken (didn't know what they were talking about) or they deliberately set forth misinformation. Who can look to teachers for "truth" after that? Similar deceptions, such as Santa Claus, the Easter bunny, Mickey Mouse and Uncle Sam, are usually amusing and harmless. On the other hand, the "all are equal" idea is potentially explosive. Operating school classes on the "equal" principle shackles the really able students to mediocrity and presses the non-students into hopeless confusion and invalidation. In industry, filling a technical or supervisory position by job title or by reference to college degree only may cause the whole mission to fail. Some skilled jobs require so much personal interest and specialized skills that only one in ten nominally qualified applicants can wear the position comfortably and produce an outstanding performance. Practical teachers and leaders know people are not equal. They find out where a person's at, and help him set realistic goals for self-realization and growth. People love to feel that they are growing. It's honest, and it's real.

*Saturation.* Too much of anything causes loss of interest, disdain, disregard, waste, devaluation, repulsion and sometimes physical illness. Too much education causes everyday affairs to seem simple and dull. Too much research into comparative religions can cause a person to lose his convictions; he may become too liberal. Too much food makes the prospects of hunger unrealistic. Too much money mocks principles of thrift. Pollution everywhere seems hopeless. Daily war news is not news; we get used to war and its horrors. Highway deaths, national debt, rising crime, bombs enough to kill everybody a hundred times? Who can take daily life or national affairs seriously?

Saturation creates a situation where the individual doesn't count. In overcrowded cities and schools individual needs must sometimes be sacrificed for the good of the masses. Personal attitudes and actions matter little. Codes of morality are arbitrary and superficial. Saturation invalidates a person's individuality.

One approach to the problems of saturation is to limit communication in those areas. Children should not be forced to go

## Invalidation

to school after a certain age, say fourteen. It might be more healthful for the kids *and* the schools if they were forced to *either* work *or* study.

Reports of national and world problems could be censored from the mass media, radio, TV and newspapers, yet be easily and accurately available in specialized publications at newsstands.

Families could be taught the benefits of budgeting allowances for food and spending money as a step towards emotional maturity. An artificial shortage of food and money could be created by promoting the desirability of seeking quality rather than quantity. Quality foods and clothes are too good to waste and much more satisfying in many ways.

*Incomplete cycles.* This is a basic principle of hangups. There seems to be a psychic law which declares that every cycle of action once begun must be finished—sometime, somewhere, somehow. "Life force" is invested in an undertaking to energize it. When the project / event / happening is finished, the force is set free, returned with interest, for possible reinvestment. Incomplete (stagnated) cycles invalidate a person, resulting in tiredness (life force is already committed and so unavailable), loss of confidence, restricted field of interest and awareness, and a sense of inadequacy or guilt.

"Incomplete cycle" means unfinished business. One style of psychotherapy owes its success to a scheme for recalling old (childhood) events which were incomplete and proceeding to complete them artificially. Such cases demonstrate dramatically that incomplete cycles can cause lifelong emotional problems.

The lesson to be learned here is to practice, and teach, the importance of ending cycles, of finishing unfinished business. For teenagers, going into the service or away to college is a dramatic way to finish childhood and commence adulthood. Mourning of a dead loved one can either be suspended for years or be systematically finished in a few weeks. Some simple argument or fight may hold a married couple at arm's length for years, yet it could be settled by an honest, painful, knock-down-drag-out fight in which the issue is won or lost once and for all. Sometimes it is good to clear the air. (See chap. 17 on healthy fights.)

Some thought should be given to starting cycles accidentally or unknowingly. Pregnancy, bodily injury, criminal record, legal liability, food poisoning, some kinds of business contracts with fine print, starting a military career—these start long, unwieldy cycles.

*"Safety is no accident."* Home and shop safety don't happen by themselves. People have to study safety, think safety, practice safe habits and procedures, create safety regulations and enforce them, record accidents and collect data for safety research projects. Likewise high morale, emotional maturity, personal responsibility and optimum human performance cannot be achieved or maintained by accident. Only a deliberate permanent program can cure emotional problems and *prevent* unnecessary suffering and losses.

Suggestions for an emotional-safety campaign:

—Advocate a return to common courtesy and professional dignity.

—Tell people it can be wrong to tease and be gruff. Some think it is cute and sociable.

—Maintain games conditions. Help people to become interested, fascinated, absorbed and challenged as regards their studies or jobs.

—Start perpetual courses to teach Emotional First Aid. A new class could start every month at a local college or health clinic.

—Provide easy access to a local emotional-counseling service. More than a crisis clinic, this clinic should be a place where people are invited to come to talk over problems and frustrations of any kind, even small ones. This service might provide a referee for family fights.

—Set good examples of validation: give compliments, awards, acknowledgments, encouragement.

Wonderful things happen to people who have learned to validate others. They practice noticing, approving, encouraging, contributing, appreciating, needing. These are emotional vitamins. As the song said, "A spoonful of sugar makes the medicine go down." The habit of validating others makes life's rough spots fewer and easier.

CHAPTER 9

## *Emotional Shock*

"Shock" is a word used in medicine to describe many varied and often unrelated abnormal conditions that affect both mind and body. There is shell shock, which is a psychiatric condition. Emotional, nervous and psychic shock are vague terms often applied to fainting. Electric shock is a definite injury, as is chemical shock, caused by poisons or by overdoses, as of insulin by diabetics.

Physical shock is a depressed state of all body functions due to failure of the circulation. It may be caused by severe bleeding, burns, crushing injuries, fractured bones. Shock occurs when there is a severe injury to any part of the body from any cause. Starvation and disease may also cause shock. Severe shock may result in death.

The Red Cross *First Aid* textbook has a very good chapter on physical shock; this material makes a good introduction to a lecture on emotional shock. *The two always occur together;* we refer to "physical" shock when the traumatic situation begins with a physical accident, and to "emotional" shock when the primary situation is emotional, with physical aftereffects.

Here are some characteristics of shock (from dictionary and Red Cross text):

—Normal functions inhibited, depressed, some degree of immobility.

—Loss of control, impaired logic, abnormal attitudes.

—Senses limited, numbness, nausea, dizziness, weakness.

*Causes.* Pain, fear, grief, sudden noise or a flash of light, a sudden loss, electric shock, powerful drugs, excessive or unusual motion, a highly emotional thought.

*Delayed symptoms.* Evidence of shock may not show up for

several hours after a causative incident. This is a very important point for several reasons:

—Immediately after the traumatic incident the person may appear normally alert and rational. He may attempt to resume his duties and responsibilities, only to collapse, perhaps at a dangerous moment should he be driving a car, climbing a ladder or walking across a busy street.

—Seeing no serious symptoms, people naturally ignore the possibility of severe shock and therefore fail to take First Aid measures. When the weakness, dizziness, cold chills, deep sighs, tears, etc., do appear, the vicious cycle of disastrous changes in the body has become operative and the patient's life is in danger.

Remember, *every injured person is potentially a patient in shock and should be regarded and treated as such, whether symptoms of shock are present or not.*

This may be virtually impossible when symptoms are not present! Active people of all ages consider it ridiculous to lie down, just in case. Getting extra heat to the body may not be easy. Workers on the job don't want to be babied as if they couldn't take it. People just don't want to take a little bump too seriously. Part of a prevention program is to teach people that shock is potentially a very serious matter and that it is wise to do whatever is necessary to avoid complications. Liken resting awhile for shock to getting a tetanus shot after stepping on a rusty nail or to rabies shots after being bitten by a dog.

"What," you may ask, "does all this have to do with Emotional First Aid?"

—Weakness, dizziness, nausea and nervous shivers certainly reduce a person's awareness and ability, diminish his self-confidence and resourcefulness, magnify his fear and anxiety.

—Conversely, a sudden loss, a fearful panic or intense anger can cause the physical symptoms.

—Familiarity with the principles of physical shock makes it easier to learn the newer, psychic principles; in a sense we are going from the known to the unknown, or at least from the familiar to the unfamiliar.

## TRAUMATIC SITUATIONS

"Trauma" means wound; a bodily injury produced by violence. A "traumatic psychosis" is a mental disorder caused by a wound or emotional violence. A similar term is "engram," meaning "a lasting, subconscious memory of a psychic (emotional) experience." "Trauma" and "engram" are sometimes used interchangeably, since every bodily wound and pain creates a simultaneous emotional shock, and every painful psychic experience is a psychic wound and causes a subconscious scar.

## ENGRAM

An engram is a subconscious scar. One of the fundamental principles of Emotional First Aid is to understand, relieve and if possible, prevent engrams. The reason is that events which are physically and emotionally painful can cause changes in personality, create phobias, allergies, compulsions, etc.

## EMOTIONAL SHOCK SYMPTOMS

Itemizing the peculiar things people do and experience under the heading of emotional shock symptoms is probably an oversimplification, offering a rule with many exceptions. This is one starting place for discussing the causes and prevention of some kinds of abnormal behavior.

—Attention and awareness greatly attenuated, thus limiting communication, learning, responsibility, concentration, etc., very short attention span.

—Logic and reason sharply impaired; errors more frequent.
—Tendency to exaggerate, misrepresent, lie.
—Unusual fears; hallucinations.
—Phobias, allergies, unexplained compulsions.
—Psychosomatic problems, nervous twitches, lack of appetite, excessive tiredness, insomnia, indigestion, offensive body odors.
—Quick temper, unpredictable moods, frequent fights.
—Occasional loss of control of bladder or bowels; may break

out in tears or laughter, or sudden hot flashes and excessive perspiration.

—Absence of motivation or ambition; no interest in games or any kind of recreation.

—Accident proneness.

—Poor ESP. Unable to sense desires and reactions of other people; unable to foresee probable results of a course of action.

—Sense of time is unreliable. Slow, often tardy, unable to visualize long-term goals.

—Lacks self-confidence. Shy, non-participating, no guts, inferiority complex, insecure.

—Sadist. Takes unusual pleasure in witnessing or causing suffering in others.

—Engrams are timeless. They may lie dormant for years, then become turned on in full force.

—They are partially or totally subconscious and unknown.

—Everyone has some. They are so common and normal that they go unnoticed. Only when they are obviously painful or embarrassing are they labeled "psychosomatic," "phobia," "allergy," etc.

—When stimulated and activated, an engram has a hypnotic-like control over emotions, attitudes and any function of the human body. *This control is involuntary and irrational.* An engram makes us do something that is unnecessary, undesirable and probably harmful. This is done either without our conscious knowledge and consent, or worse, against our will.

—Any one of a wide selection of details in the original traumatic event may become a trigger, or pushbutton, capable of stimulating or turning on a psychic replay, with possible overtones from similar later events. The word pushbutton seems very appropriate here; everybody knows how automatic pushbuttons work on radios, auto transmissions, elevators, washing machines, etc. people have pushbuttons too.

—There may be a time delay of minutes, hours or days between pushing the psychic button and getting the replay action. Research was delayed for years until this delay factor was discovered.

## Emotional Shock

—Engrams can be thought of as super 3-D movies, with stereo sound tracks, and up to fifty other tracks for simultaneously recording and playing back smell, pain, time, temperature, emotions, attitudes, inner thoughts, etc. These movies can be slowed down, speeded up, run backwards, edited and dubbed in. Some run in color, some in black and white.

—Usually the engram is played back without the picture, which is one reason few people realize that this phenomenon is part of their daily lives. They seem to hear the voices, feel the emotions and follow the compulsive patterns, but the picture is black. This is about as confusing as listening to a TV set with the picture turned off. Actually it is more like watching a show on one channel and hearing the audio from another. No wonder people have trouble communicating, learning, following instructions and living together.

—Our subconscious is recording the events of our lives continuously, automatically, even when we are unconscious from injury, anesthetic or amnesia.

—All events of your life are cross-referenced and indexed. Under ideal conditions memory circuits can recall all associated events and data in fractions of a second. Evaluations and computations are made almost instantly—subconsciously, of course.

—Engrams (recordings of shock situations) play back misinformation and data which are no longer timely or appropriate. The key to our emotional problems is that our subconscious problem-solving computer accepts the engrammatic data as valid, which they most certainly are not. Thus we find ourselves making wrong decisions, doing foolish things, having sick bodies, etc.

—Engrams absorb psychic energy. It seems to be locked on the movie sound track. Engrams make people tired. Therapy unlocks the energy and helps people feel more alive. Each person seems to have been born with a certain amount of psychic energy (life force?). As engrams accumulate through his lifetime, his drive and ambition fade. He gets tired easily. His energy is stored, locked in, hung up in his engrams. Also, some engrams have the hypnotic-like command to be tired.

—Engrammatic energy causes physical changes in human

bodies (and plants, according to Dr. Clive Backster) which can be detected and recorded with electronic instruments such as the "lie-detector" polygraph, ohmmeter, E meter and electroencephalograph.

—Psychic energy is locked in an engram by a secret—that is, by details of the traumatic event which are unknown to the person. When he learns the secret, the energy is unlocked and the engram is converted to a memory, and the energy is made available for use in daily life (present time).

—Engrams can be converted into harmless memories by various therapy procedures, processes and drills. Classic psychoanalysis and hypnotic regression are well-documented schemes, for instance. They are too complicated for amateur Emotional First Aid, however.

—The engram secret can be unlocked by (1) finding (recalling) the original traumatic incident in the subconscious records and (2) showing its movie over and over until the secret unlocks. At the end of the seemingly endless repetition the person "cognites" on the secret and knows that the engram is discharged by his sense of inner relief and the feeling of energy being released. He feels good again.

—If such a therapeutic cycle is stopped mid-cycle, the person may be hung up in the movie, out of present-time reality and very uncomfortable. He is in his movie, and it concerns events that happened some other place and some other time. This condition is not dangerous; it will wear off in an hour or two, or a day or so. To prevent such unnecessary discomfort, the cycle should always be completed once started.

—Like an automatic washer an engram can have its button pushed, go through its cycle and reset itself for the next time endlessly. It may wait months or years doing nothing, just waiting for the button to be pushed. Only, engrams don't rust; they are timeless and can last forever. Psychoanalysis has proved that in some cases the original traumatic incident which caused the engram happened decades ago in some childhood event.

Summarizing, emotional shock is caused by a violent emotional or physical event. Shock causes a wide variety of disabilities and

## Emotional Shock

discomforts, ranging in seriousness from light to lethal, and may cause undesirable changes in personality. Shock symptoms may not appear for minutes or hours after the traumatic incident. An emotional shock causes an engram, a subconscious phenomenon capable of causing undesirable effects for the rest of a lifetime.

## PREVENTION

A study of actual case histories provides clues for preventing emotional disorders:

—It is impossible to prevent *all* traumatic situations in real life. An interesting exciting life must have challenges and risks. Most people play the odds in the game of life so close that they lose part of the time, thus creating potentially traumatic situations.

—Resistance to shock varies widely. Age is a factor: a strong, healthy adult can tolerate violence that would cause shock in the young, the old or the feeble. Pain, hunger, confusion, frustration or a sudden loss reduces resistance to shock. Excessive cold, heat, motion or fatigue increases susceptibility.

—A seemingly normal, harmless event as seen by an adult may appear to be personal disaster to a child.

—*Any* detail or point of interest in a traumatic event may become a pushbutton capable of turning on future emotional disturbances. Words, thoughts, sounds, smells, time of day, *anything*, can become the index tab recalling portions of the incident years hence.

## COMMON TRAUMATIC SITUATIONS

—Physical pain, illness, infection, severe cold or heat.
—Sudden noise, flashes of light, motion.
—Frustration, failure, loss.
—Cruel jokes, horseplay, overwhelming (bullying).
—Confusion, overcomplexity, misinformation (such as lies).
—Strong emotional events: harsh anger, despair, grief, stark fear.
—Starved for psychic income: deep hunger for love, ap-

preciation, warm companionship, sense of personal worth, being wanted.

—Enforced unreality: harsh environment, unreasonable commands, injustice, undeserved punishment.

—Environment changing too fast (confusing) or too slow (boring).

—Proximity to traumatic conditions of others. Call it empathy, sympathy or psychic induction, it is easy to feel sadness at a funeral and anger while standing in an angry mob.

—Guilt: self-condemnation for being wicked, deserving punishment.

—Shame: loss of self-esteem, disgraced, degraded, humiliated.

—Powerful negative suggestion made by one in authority.

## SAMPLE CASE HISTORY

Sixteen-year-old John put down his funnybook and decided to try the prank he had just read about. After putting catsup and grease on his four-year-old sister, he picked her up to carry her in the house. "Pretend to be asleep," he told her. "Mother will think you've been hurt, and we'll surprise her with our trick." He rushed into the house with his sister in his arms shouting, "Mother, Mother, it's Judy!"

Mother dropped the saucepan of soup, burning her legs. Lurching backward in pain, she burned her rump on the kitchen stove. Starting to run toward her "bleeding" baby, she slipped on the spilled soup and fell to the floor with a thump. Her wrist was severely sprained as she tried instinctively to break the fall. Sobbing, she crawled to the table and scrambled to her feet, determined to get to her injured child.

The teenager realized his little drama had turned into a disaster. The soup was spilled, the floor was a mess, his mother was hurt. He knew that he was in trouble.

When Judy opened her eyes and smiled, and Mother suddenly realized the facts of the hoax, a new traumatic incident began. Incident No. 1 had started with great concern for Judy's pain. Incident No. 2 started with the realization that her pain and

# Emotional Shock

clumsiness were wasted, and that she had acted foolishly. She had been made the victim of a cruel prank.

Most of what happened in the kitchen was her own fault. She had jumped to the conclusion that Judy was maimed or killed, and had not checked the facts. Had the accident been real, John had brought Judy to her for help, and she had betrayed his faith by "losing her cool." Finally, custom demanded that she hold John responsible for causing the whole mess with malice aforethought and ugly intent. How could she punish him for causing her pain?

*Observations.*

—John and Judy created a game, probably hoping to attract Mother's attention and admiration. Their childish inexperience could not foresee Mother's panic. This prank was similar to bringing snakes and small animals in Mother's presence for dramatic effect.

—Mother over-responded. We might guess that her subconscious equated Judy's injuries with the horrors of other accidents in years past. Her subconscious seemed to exclaim, "Oh! Oh! It's happened again! Every time this happens we scream and faint!" At least we presume that she didn't consciously decide that the best thing to do was scream, drop soup and then sit in it.

—Mother *thought* Judy was badly injured. It wasn't true, we know, but the *thought* caused emotional and physical shock.

—An optimum response to Judy's bloody condition would have been: (1) "What happened?" (2) Lay her down. (3) Determine the exact nature of the injuries. (4) Call a doctor if necessary. (5) Stop the bleeding.

—See what shock does for self-control and the ability to do what must be done! Mother knew that a soup kettle drops if not held securely, but she dropped it. She knew that the hot stove was a few inches behind her, but she backed into it. She knew that soup makes a floor slippery, but she slipped anyhow. She knew John couldn't cause her to do these things, but she blamed him. (He accidentally started the sequence, but once Mother went into shock, she was on her own.)

Chagrin and embarrassment over the incident may linger for

the rest of her life. She will develop a thing about pranksters and practical jokes. She may decide that John is a cruel, thoughtless boy and treat him accordingly the rest of her life. She may become allergic to catsup.

The reader can apply these principles to analyze cases of emotional shock in school, home, office or shop. Watch for these factors:

—Moment of crisis in which reality drops out, usually signaled by physical pain or great anxiety.

—Individual events illustrating unreality, that is, foolish actions.

—Person's probable unrealistic appraisal of the situation.

—Examples of miscommunication.

—Possible permanent effects to self and others.

There are a thousand ways to act crazy, and emotional shock can cause them all. There are other possible causes, such as brain damage, birth defects, hypnosis, powerful drugs and malnutrition. Some emotional shock is preventable by practicing common sense and courtesy. Some shock symptoms are curable by psychotherapy. Side effects from accompanying loss of reason and physical control can be minimized by recognizing shock-causing situations and taking precautionary measures.

# CHAPTER 10

# *Self-image*

"Who are you?" This question is asking for your name, something about some of the people you know and a hint about where you live. "Who do you think you are?" enunciated in a crisp, slightly acid tone means, "I think you have behaved too boldly and assumed rights or responsibililties far beyond your authority." Technically the first question asks, "What role are you playing?"

Everyone has a self-image, whether he knows it or not. Many questions must be answered to learn about a person's self-image. "How do you see yourself? Do you like your name? How do you feel about the guy you see in the mirror? Do you believe that you can do anything anybody else can do? Are you the kind of person you want to be? If your daily life was to be made part of a movie, how would you describe the character you play? What would you do if you could do *anything* you wanted to? Do you think that your parents and close friends know the real you?"

## IMPORTANCE OF SELF-IMAGE IN EMOTIONAL FIRST AID

People who see themselves as potential leaders and feel that they are growing toward maturity will be more likely to offer aid than to need it. Those who have not visualized themselves in satisfactory roles and who feel unlovely and unlucky will be in frequent need of all manner of social services and aids.

Self-image counseling guides character and personality development. The counselor can create the opportunity to crystallize moral concepts, personal standards, social attitudes and long-term social and economic goals.

A student might not decide to do something special or to seek a satisfying goal without coaching from a counselor. He might never get a vision of a future happy situation for himself unless someone offers him such a role. Hope and motivation do not come easy to those who are brought up in a hopeless environment.

Is "We are what we have to be" true?

Is it true that you can't change human nature? If by human nature we mean "behavior patterns suitable for, and determined by, the self-image," then it is true: a person's personality and character are fixed and predetermined. He must play a certain role *until he is given a different part* (until he develops a different self-image). Isn't this the basic principle of the pre-school "head start program"?

"I get to know who I am and how much I am worth by what I see happen out there." Responses of the environment are important in establishing character and self-image. Since a child's environment is controlled by parents, teachers and relatives, they must understand the principles involved. Many don't, and they are busily undermining their children's emotional foundations. Metacom is a factor (see discussion of metacom in chapter 5).

"Self-image" is a topical term which includes several other self-awareness concepts:

| | | |
|---|---|---|
| —Self-pity | —Self-realization | —Self-control |
| —Self-discipline | —Self-confidence | —Self-consciousness |
| —Self-defense | —Self-denial | —Self-respect |
| —Self-determination | —Modesty | —Conceit |
| —Self-sufficiency | —Self-sacrifice | —Pride |

Career counselors ask stock questions intended to help students search within themselves for answers.

—Who are you?
—What are you doing now?
—What would you like to do in the future?
—What obstacles do you foresee to keep you from that future?
—How might you overcome those obstacles?
—Why does that future seem desirable?
—Can you think of some alternate goals?

## EXAMPLES OF BAD SELF-IMAGE

The little voice inside says, "I'm not good enough," "I can't," "Nobody cares," "I couldn't care less."

*Self-image* 69

Shame: he doesn't like his own name, body, face, clothes, family. Misfit: "I'll show them!" "I don't hafta if I don't wanna." *These are powerful emotions!*

## A PERSONAL STANDARD OF EXCELLENCE*

Why should you have lofty goals? Who wants to be eager and look ahead and become a professional man, able to do a professional job? Why knock yourself out to get an extra license or diploma or learn an extra skill? Who cares?

Who cares!

Should somebody care? Should you be a "good boy" to please someone? Is that a good reason for doing less than your best—because you think no one is watching?

Whom would you like for an audience while you perform? Whom do you want to *care?* Are you prepared to put on a good show *right now* if someone cares?

I know you don't shirk your duty; you are not a coward. You are a good sport, and you wouldn't actually cheat. You like to be on a team that does things and goes places; you want to do your part on that team.

I know that you know what mistakes you make before others tell you. You'll agree, I'm sure, that you are far from being a champ, that there is lots of room for improvement. Actually you would be mighty pleased to have more skill and ability. You would like to be a winner and a leader. It would be fine to have others look to you because of your willingness, your resourcefulness and your cheerful cooperation.

You have average intelligence—which you keep in neutral gear a lot of the time. When was the last time you *really tried*, really put all of yourself into a project, and when you finished, stood back and said, "There, I did that"?

Surely the ace athlete has to put in his practice and hard work *before* anybody notices, or cares. Who ever heard of any big league team signing up a pitcher *before* he spent hundreds of hours learning to throw the ball?

---
* An essay.

Why not decide to *be somebody!* Be a man, and learn to do a man's job. Don't ask someone else if you are doing okay. *Ask yourself.* When you become as good as you know you can be, someone *will* care.

\* \* \*

Imagine an educational scheme of the future which would provide each student with an optimum vision of personal social and economic goals. Each student would see himself on a ladder climbing, learning to become his best self, feeling himself grow.

Teachers would coach him in self-evaluation, motivation and goal seeking. They would monitor his progress and help him maintain a games condition meaningful to him and acceptable to society.

"Of course," you say. "We are doing this." Look again at the gradient scale! Whether we are discussing vocational training, physical health or emotional maturity, "average" is only halfway up! Only a few are in the optimum area. From one point of view *half the students are below average.* This may mean that millions of students will miss their chance to become emotionally mature adults. They won't know what they are missing, but they will sense vaguely that others are happy and they are not. Their lives will be filled with hostility, fears, self-pity and apathy. These are the powerful emotions of immaturity.

A good self-image is:

—a source of pride and self-respect.

—an automatic pilot: error-correcting (conscience) and goal-seeking (ambition).

—an internal standard of excellence; voluntary morality.

## SUGGESTIONS FOR PREVENTING NEGATIVE SELF-IMAGE

—Grownups should check each other for negative metacom.

—On-the-spot analysis and therapy can prevent temporary emotional upsets from becoming permanent (chap. 9).

—Avoid negative environments (chap. 7).

## SUGGESTIONS FOR CREATING A POSITIVE SELF-IMAGE

—Purposefully plan ways to ensure that your child gets the messages and impressions you want him to have. Create growing situations. Ask questions to direct his thinking and help him to decide what he believes and why. When a person arrives at a conclusion himself, he is more inclined to accept its validity than if the same idea is bluntly expounded to him in an authoritative manner.

—When possible, help him to perform successfully: to play with kids his own age, to be enrolled in a school class which is not too hard or too easy. Don't expect too much or too little of him.

—Good contemporary models. Close association with other people who are courageous, fair, helpful, purposeful and fun makes it easy to be and do likewise. Generally we can select our own friends and aid in the selection of childhood playmates.

—Good books, movies and TV shows guide our attitudes. We pick up strong impressions from successful biographies and from heroes in adventure stories.

—On-the-spot amateur counseling. Help a person to examine a negative attitude to see more clearly what is going on, and help him to select an *appropriate* response. Teach rational analysis of adverse situations. Discourage negative attitudes which come with emotional outbursts.

—Church, scouts and other clubs and organizations are intended to build character and train inspirational leaders.

—Self-improvement programs. One way to become more efficient at helping others to find themselves is to work on yourself. This is a satisfying adventure even if you are not a student counselor.

## CHAPTER 11

# *Control, Freedom, Security*

"Control" means:

—Deliberate, systematic planning; practical predetermined action.

—Disciplined, trained, skilled to perform with precision.

—Purposeful, reliable authority, confident, effective.

—To direct, check, regulate, dominate, restrain, start, steer, stop, command, change precisely.

Being controlled is:

—Doing what you're told, obeying commands, following directions.

—Behaving yourself, using good sense, good habits, courtesy.

—Obeying the law/rules, playing fair.

—Practicing skills, training, drilling, studying enough.

—Self-control, self-discipline, making yourself do what you should.

"Freedom" means to be:

—Unrestricted.

—Independent.

—Enjoying all privileges.

—Without restraint.

—Exempt from laws, regulations, responsibilities, *control*.

"Security" means to be:

—Safe.

—Guaranteed of survival.

—Well protected.

—Without fear or doubt.

Emotional problems arise from *bad* control, such as cruel slavery, a harsh dictatorship or a wicked stepmother. No control causes problems too. Too many choices may cause frustration and confusion. No useful work or satisfying games can be had without good control.

## Control, Freedom, Security

Low-scale people resist control. They say that schools, social customs and strict parents violate their freedom. Complaining that they are oppressed, they drop out of school, scoff at courtesy and customs and mock the advice of parents. Refusing to be controlled, they have narrowed their choices of action (freedom). Lamenting that math and science courses are too laborious, and boring, they step into an adult world qualified only as helpers or assemblers or for other menial tasks of the most monotonous sort *for the rest of their lives.*

High-scale students control easily. They accept authority gracefully, but on the other hand, parents and teachers tend to be more lenient and indulgent. Those who accept rules and regulations without chafing *are trusted with more freedom.* Those who persevere through endless hours of classes and homework to graduate find a wide selection of jobs, as well as opportunities for more education and advancement.

Low-scale people who demand their rights to do as they damn please and jeer at the law often find themselves in jail or the hospital. Freedom is not the right to do anything that comes into your head. It is a privilege which must be earned, a privilege which permits a person to make a reasonable choice.

Some parents are hung up with two axioms that "everybody knows" (but that aren't true): (1) "Children will always make good decisions based on logic and common sense." (2) "It is cruel to whip a child and insist on his performance and strict obedience." These parents are raising rascals who irritate teachers, make Grandma nervous, chafe at military service and grumble about their civilian jobs. Rather than try to be "nice" to their child, parents should instill into his little head: "Wherever you go there will be someone to tell you what to do [authority], and there will be rules [customs, laws]. Your job is to find out Who's in charge here? and What are the rules?" Babies who learn these two questions never have a problem getting their share of freedom and security from parents, teachers and bosses.

It seems that all the good things in life come from good control and all the bad things in life come from bad control or no control at all. Some emotional problems could be prevented by identifying bad situations and teaching people good control skills.

*Gradient scale of controlling others*:
—"Light touch" makes authoritative suggestions.
—Clear, reasonable directives.
—Casual hints (indirect, incomplete).
—Sharp, hostile commands.
—Shouts, curses, force; frequent errors.
—Vague orders with threats.
—Pleading.
—No attempt at control (apathy).

The idea that freedom is wonderfully valuable is the result of bad control. "Freedom" is getting away from slavery and oppression. People experiencing good control do not seek freedom. They love and respect their leader. Their duties are meaningful. Rules are clearly seen to be purposeful and just. They sense the security of belonging in this area of good control; they are members of a team who enjoy working and playing together.

"Freedom" is no control. It cannot bring security. No control implies no plans or systems; random, accidental, fortuitous events; only meager instinctive skills; leadership and authority, if any, established by force. "Freedom" is somewhat dangerous.

Good control is important to good games and security. It is critical in emotional health. Many kinds of emotional problems solve as if by magic when an authoritative figure arrives on the scene and establishes law and order, whether in family affairs, in the classroom or on the job.

Why, then, does over half the population resist good control? People don't resist *good* control. They don't know what it is. They never had any! They resist *bad* control. At their level on the emotional scale that is all there is—bad control. To them the word control stirs ugly reflections of other highly emotional terms, such as being shoved around, getting caught and punished, being forced to work at menial tasks, endure drudgery and boredom, restrictions: "You can't have, can't do, stay out." Of course they

*Control, Freedom, Security*

seek freedom from bad control. No one has told them that what they really want is *good* control.

## PREVENTION OF BAD CONTROL

—Analyze typical situations, define terms.

—Advocate strict enforcement of good control; teach that good discipline is vital education.

—Re-establish the absolute authority of parents and teachers.

—Teach that painful discipline is not cruel. Nature inflicts pain, even death, on creatures that are thoughtless or careless. The term "mature responsibility" implies that you had better care about what goes on, you had better do what you are doing right, *or you will be sorry*. The term "discipline" implies that pain of some sort will surely follow mistakes. Children need to know this.

—Try to create and maintain high-scale conditions on all dynamics.

# CHAPTER 12

# *Psycho-cybernetics*[*]

"Cybernetics" (from the Greek, "the steersman") is the science of man's built-in servo-mechanism which performs as a guidance system toward goal-targets, a sort of electronic brain for setting up and solving problems of living. It is the harnessing of man's abilities to visualize future satisfactory games and states of being. It is the science of motivation. It is the scheme for utilizing communication, games, self-image, control, etc., to create a successful life.

Psycho-cybernetics is a new space-age word for a principle that has long been known by such terms as positive thinking; T.N.T.: The Creative Power Within You; auto-hypnosis; faith; prayer dynamics.

Applied to Emotional First Aid, psycho-cybernetics teaches: "Keep your eye on what we are trying to do here. Visualize the whole program gathering steam, working to prevent unnecessary emotional suffering everywhere. Don't worry about details. So you are not a teacher or psychiatrist. So what if there is no mental health clinic in your town. Think about it. Talk about it. Read about it. Hope for it. Get ready for it. Visualize it so clearly that you can feel it. Keep it on your mind. This is how to make dreams come true.

Study the biographies of sports champions and famous inventors. This was their basic formula: dream, study, work—dream, study, work. Visualize an exciting goal; learn all the technical details, then search for opportunities.

---

[*] For some of this chapter I am indebted to Maxwell Maltz, M.D., *Psycho-cybernetics*, p. 17 *et passim*.

## NEGATIVE CYBERNETICS WORKS TOO!

"It isn't that I'm lazy. I'm just not motivated." What a fancy excuse for doing nothing! It is a real problem, though—letting the months and years slip by in vaguely disturbed apathy. It's a no-game condition. You can't feel good about doing nothing.

What makes people *go,* anyhow? Why do some people *want* to study and work and build and stick their necks out?

Pictures. People make pictures in their minds. A wife might make a picture of a pretty flower garden. A teenage girl might picture a formal dance and a lovely gown. A young fellow might picture a hot rod. What is one of your favorite pictures?

You probably haven't noticed that these pictures are in 3-D and may even have color and sound and other sensations. But the most important thing you put in your pictures is *you.* You move yourself into your picture and sort of try it on to see how it feels. If it feels good, you'll begin to "make it solid."

A good engineer can visualize a new machine and actually *try it out.* He rejects many plans as unworkable because the picture trials just don't seem right. Housewives can "see" how a new dress will look before they buy the material.

Good pictures have created symphonies, skyscrapers and jet planes. Conversely, muzley, grookey pictures have warped lives and corroded personalities.

Cowards seldom really get hurt; they just look at dangerous pictures and "see" that they might get hurt. A bum may look at pictures of being tired. An alcoholic may look at a picture of himself being scolded.

As often as not the grookey pictures are black. You can't *see* a thing, just feel. Black pictures are the worst; you don't even realize that a picture is supposed to be there, except that all the rest of what goes with it is there: feeling bad, tiredness, lack of interest, perhaps a vague fear. Sometimes the sound comes through; a little voice seems to say, "Who cares?" or "It isn't worth it."

You may not believe in fortune-telling, but you *can* begin to create your own future. It's easy. *Sort your pictures.* Keep the ones you would like to have come true. When ugly pictures show themselves, crowd them out by making some good ones. What you read about, talk about, think about and dream about are important. They are the plans for your future. Make them clear and exciting and—and any way you want them!

## PICTURE POWER/TIGER DRILL

This is a psychological game (it's fun). It is also a scheme for boosting psychic power. The idea is to recall a time when you were really happy and successful and confident that you had a certain situation firmly under control. Recall a moment; get a clear mental-image picture *with you in it*; then feel again how successful you felt.

Here are the rules for this game:

1. Person No. 1 says: "Recall a moment of success."

2. Person No. 2 does so, describing the situation in a sentence or two.

3. Person No. 1 says: "Okay. Now, repeat something nice that someone said or thought about your success."

4. Person No. 2 does so.

5. Person No. 1 says: "Okay" or "Fine," to indicate, "I perceive that you have done as I asked. End of cycle."

6. Steps 1–5 are one cycle. The game is to repeat the cycle ten or fifteen times. Most people are inclined to want to find a new moment each time, but newness is not required. It is okay to mention the same moment more than once.

7. If he gets stuck, ask him what the word success means to him. After he defines success, go back to "Recall a moment of success" again.

8. Don't get sidetracked into interesting discussions or comparing notes. Just keep looking at and feeling of pictures of success until Person No. 2 is feeling bold and venturesome.

It is easily demonstrated that mental-image pictures may have strong emotional impact. The emotions may be pleasant and constructive, or they may bring discomfort and confusion. Mental-image pictures may be memories of past events, or visions of pure fiction such as might be created by a movie or TV show, or they may have little other basis than imagination. For instance, we can daydream about wondrous adventures; we can also worry about possibly dangerous future events.

Much emotional suffering could be prevented by teaching people to sort their pictures, keeping only the pictures of success.

## CHAPTER 13

# Stable Data, Meaningful Truth

Let's start with some definitions.

*Stable*: standing firmly, not easily moved or changed, durable, reliable, steadfast, inflexible, permanent. *Data*: authoritative reference points; facts; natural elements; bits of information. *Stable data*: a reliable reference system on which to build. Natural laws, geometric axioms, engineering principles, "facts of life," geodetic bench marks, religious dogma (for some people.) *Axiom*: a self-evident statement, a "thinking tool," a natural law. An axiom is explained and proved once clearly in a basic text, then presumed to be a self-evident truth in all future discussions. *Truth*: hard fact; reality, agreed-upon opinions, beliefs which agree with and explain lesser facts, reliable data. *Meaningful*: significant, makes sense, interesting, acceptable, understandable, useful, clarifies or answers a question. *Meaningful truth*: an idea, fact or other communication of such a gradient that the receiver can easily duplicate it. Ideas that seem to be valuable and appropriate.

Several types of emotional problems develop from inadequate stable data. Confusion, uncertainty, lack of motivation, immorality and tiredness are a few examples.

Consider the stable datum "Somebody cares; it does matter what I do." Suddenly nobody cares! The boyfriend found a new girlfriend. The teacher scolded me for something I didn't do. My parents are too busy getting a divorce to care about me. I can't find a job. Jesus didn't answer my prayer. I broke the law and didn't get caught.

Examples of stable data references: North Star and compass for determining geographical directions; 440-cycle "A" pitch for tuning musical instruments; freezing and boiling temperatures of water determine 0 and 100 degrees on the centigrade thermometer. Science and industry would be lost without reliable standards of measurement.

People get lost, too, without their points of reference. When

## Stable Data, Meaningful Truth

the last reference point becomes obscured, people begin to spin. They lose their sense of values; they do crazy things which may change the course of their lives; their very personalities may flip.

—The sudden death of a beloved spouse.

—Being wiped out by a natural disaster, such as a flood or hurricane taking a home and business, a lifetime's work.

—Losing a bitterly fought case in court.

—Or, surprisingly, suddenly finding themselves in the clear with no enemies, no problems and plenty of money.

These are signs of emotional instability: 'Who cares?" "What difference does it make?" "I couldn't care less." "Nothing matters any more." "Nothing can be done." These phrases mean that someone's personal world is being badly shaken.

Reference points can be re-established quite easily. Unlike the scientific standards of reference which are precise and rock-bound, the stable data required by the subconscious are subjective and may differ widely from individual to individual. What seems good and very worthwhile to a teenage girl may seem to be foolish nonsense to a fifty-year-old man. A person does not need to know what eternal truth is in order to help a friend find his bearings.

A second encouraging factor is that the subconscious is very lenient about the relative values of stable data. A fact is a fact is a fact is a fact. Fact No. 1 might be: "I have decided to finish college." Fact No. 2 might be: "I will mow the lawn today." Fact No. 3 might be: "At least my dog loves me." Fact No. 4 might be: "I must eat something or I will get sick." The common value of such various "facts" is that each seems real, each seems to hold still in relation to the spinning emotions.

Here are some Emotional First Aid procedures for re-establishing emotional reference points:

—Count your blessings. So something pretty important has gone wrong. Name some things that are still right.

—Mention something you are certain of. Mention about twenty certainties. Little things will do, such as "I am certain I am breathing air" or "I am certain I have clothes on." The subconscious counts how *many,* not how significant.

# GRADIENT SCALE OF TRUTH

"Truth" is different things to different people. It is astonishing to observe men arguing whether "black" is "white." It is probably a shade of gray!

|    | Emotion Being Expressed | Accuracy of Comprehension | Values Truth | Communicates Truth | Grades of Truth |
|----|---|---|---|---|---|
| 12 | Eager | Intuitive truth | Places high value | Complete, accurate | Obviously true |
| 11 | Strong Interest | Perfect insight | on perfect accuracy, | in every detail | Systematic |
| 10 | | Authoritative | research, logic, theory, formulas, adequate records | Never misunderstood Volunteers timely info. Systematic updating | Logical Self-evident |
| 9 | Some Interest | Well informed | Generally realizes | Corrects | Academic theories |
| 8 | | Corrects errors | the value of facts | misinformation | Reasonable postulates |
| 7 | Content | Technically accurate Accepts authority | Records are bare minimum. Satisfied with approximations | Usually satisfactory | Partial evidence Recorded data |
| 6 | Bored Indifferent | Compulsive changer | Denounces research | Erratic communica. | Intuitive guesses |
| 5 | | Super critical | Solves problems by | Selective, biased | Memory |
| 4 | Hostility | Hostile to authority | cut and try Substitutes force and action for T. | Opinionated Weighed with hostility | Negative data: what can't work, can't be done, dangerous |
| 3 | Anger Tricky | Limited comprehension, | Denies truth Garbles facts | Tells lies Exaggerates | Sounds good but always wrong. |
| 2 | Fear | Tunnel vision, Mostly errors, badly distorted | Outshouts logic | Forgets Jams data systems | Garbled gibberish Imaginary, |
| 1 | Apathy | None | What is truth??? | Doesn't own try | Lies |

—Start doing some manual work. Mow the lawn. Clean house. Wash the car. Do the laundry. The harder you work, the better you'll feel.

To prevent unnecessary emotional suffering:

—Point out (teach) stable data check points for children, workers, spouses.

—Cherish and protect stable data. Don't allow broken rules to go unnoticed or unpunished. See that extra work and diligence *is* worth while.

—Establish, and insist on, Standard Operating Procedures (S.O.P.). "When this problem comes up, we always do this." Experience can be a good teacher. S.O.P.'s are specialized stable data.

It is fashionable to shoot down traditional morals, ethics and basic values. Professors seem to delight in smothering young Christians in comparative-religion classes. Several radical groups are trying to shout down the capitalist system. Public vulgarity is on the rise in the name of freedom. Parental authority over, and responsibility for, teenagers is declining. Easy credit and inflation make the principle of thrift obsolete. Do these sudden changes in the rules and attitudes contribute to the emotional problems of the nation?

## MEANINGFUL TRUTH

Stable data are meaningful truths, but a meaningful truth is not necessarily a stable datum. There are lots of truths which are not used as basic reference points. Even more important, most true facts are virtually *useless!* Too many facts are a handicap. You can get smothered in data. Some people are actually overeducated. Degrees they may have—but not in subjects which concern practical everyday living. Owning an electronics textbook with five hundred pages full of true statements may be of little help in repairing your color TV set. Five pages would be enough if they answered your questions and needs.

A truth, to be properly evaluated, must be related to another truth of equal magnitude. This means that you must almost understand something before I can explain it to you. If you can't understand what I am trying to tell you, my message is not *meaningful,* interesting or useful.

Successful interpersonal experiences depend on exchanging *meaningful* communications. Trite? Analyze some emotional problems to determine whether communications were inappropriate or inadequate. The art of counseling is re-establishing meaningful communications.

There are five kinds of truth:

*Present-time truth.* Facts that you can re-establish, recheck, or prove again by experiment or observation.

*Past-time truth.* Facts that must have been true in order that present conditions might exist but are no longer true. For example, if you come across ashes and bits of charcoal, you can confidently state that there has been a fire.

*Postulated truth.* Facts, theories or data that are postulated in order to explain or justify observable facts. Geometry proofs, electronic theory, atomic theory and some legal conclusions must be true, or the other data won't be coherent. Logic can arrive at apparent truth.

*Agreed-upon truth.* Agreement of two witnesses can establish a legal "fact." Many of our beliefs are based on the unchallenged opinions of parents, teachers, churches, books, etc.

*Intuitive sense of truth.* Sensing or feeling truth; common sense, sixth sense, knowingness, ESP. People have the experience of reading a religious article, or perhaps a legal paper, and mentally objecting to almost every point the author makes. An experienced engineer or businessman can study a design or a business deal and quickly decide whether it "feels" sound and profitable. We all expect our friends to just know when they are being kidded with obvious fiction presented with a straight face.

Intuitive knowing is a natural skill common among high-scale people. There are psychological "sensitivity drills," practice exercises which increase this skill remarkably. Very able people are said to have a "keen mind," "genius," a "gift."

The recognition and cultivation of this inner reference can be of considerable importance in a discussion of emotional maturity. Under ideal conditions this skill would:

*Stable Data, Meaningful Truth*

—Help a person avoid trickery, accidents, bad investments, etc.

—Help him make the best of several choices.

—Help him plan more skillfully and therefore be more successful.

—Regarding morals, he could more easily foresee the possible outcome of his acts and attitudes and thus be more responsible.

—He could easily tune in on the reality level of others so that his communications would be skillful and meaningful. This would make him highly valued as friend, teacher and counselor.

—In weighing controversial issues, arguments and apparent contradictions, this inner sense helps him feel a satisfactory decision quickly, thus avoiding confusion and frustration. This skill is useful in high-speed sports and driving in heavy traffic.

*The Big Lie.* A stable datum or a meaningful "truth" occasionally does not correspond to fact, yet works very well. Santa Claus and the Easter bunny seem to be practical fictions. Politics, economics and religion each have their own brand of double talk. This is, after all, why lying is considered so sinful; a good little white lie may work better than a distasteful truth. Con men and shysters prey on trusting suckers with stories that are meaningful but not true. A hypnotist can give his subject commands which are meaningful but not true. In divorce proceedings it is common to swear to claims of cruelty which are ridiculous, but since over 80 percent of divorce cases are uncontested, the false claims fulfill the legal requirements.

Assumed data are dangerous. An "intelligent guess" may be a mile off. People often think that they know and understand what is required, when actually they don't know what they don't know, which is plenty.

## APPLICATION OF STABLE-DATA PRINCIPLE TO EMOTIONAL HEALTH

1. One definition of sanity: "the ability to tolerate confusion and to recognize a stable datum."
2. Some causes of emotional problems:

—Failure to deliberately and systematically establish stable data needed for a situation.
—Permitting undesirable stable data to become established.
—Failure to protect and preserve existing desirable stable data.

3. Most people want to be good and do right, but they don't know how. They cannot see clearly what is needed.

4. Contradicting authorities invalidate their data, causing confusion, frustration, indifference and postponement of decisions and actions.

Examples:
—Parents who disagree on discipline for children.
—Political candidates who call each other names.
—Scientists who debate the pros and cons of fluoridation, atomic energy, vitamins, organic gardening, pollution control, etc.
—Religious "authorities" who argue logic and scriptures.

Hearing both sides of every question may be democratic and just, but it is very expensive in time and effort and may abort the mission, that is, end in a stalemate. Prompt, efficient, suitable action may be more desirable than academic debates.

5. A common expression: people who have lost sight of their stable data are said to be spinning (acting crazy). The spinning can be quickly corrected by helping these people re-establish a feeling of certainty about something, almost anything.

6. People often believe things that aren't true. Using false data can create emotional stress. Early counseling can correct false data and prevent unnecessary emotional suffering.

CHAPTER 14

# *Religion*

Religion is a meaningful belief in supernatural beings.

The relative merits of various denominations, articles of faith, dogmas and orthodox doctrines will be avoided in this chapter. Most people are exposed to some sort of religious teaching. A large number of people have powerful emotional experiences based on religious beliefs. It is hoped that the following ideas will encourage group discussions and that religious teachers will find ways to accentuate the positive and eliminate the negative.

## RELIGION AS AN EMOTIONAL STABILIZER

*Moral code.* Every religion sets forth a code of conduct for its members. The Ten Commandments is one such code. If a person voluntarily accepts the rules and doctrines of a church, he promises to try to practice self-control, fair play and cooperative brotherhood and to strive toward emotional maturity. Each church insists that it *does* matter what you do, and even what you think.

*Belief in a deity.* Believing in God, who sees all, knows all and is all-powerful, is a mixed blessing. Believers feel confident that they are never alone, that God is watching and recording every thought and deed and that eventually the books will be balanced and punishments or rewards will be assigned. This is a widely held belief and may well be the nucleus of all religions. Believers are motivated to be good according to their own standards (conscience), even when nobody is looking, "because God cares."

*Church-centered activities.* In many communities the local church is one of two social centers, the other being the local pub. Both ward off loneliness. There are many fringe benefits in addition to the main idea of worship. Choir, scouts, philosophical discussion groups and social action circles offer opportunities for self-improvement, wholesome fun and plans for contributing to others in the community. The local church usually has a planned, authorized program of activities in progress, sustained by tradition. If this kind of community center did not exist, people would be deprived of social, growing and sometimes therapeutic situations.

## TOO MUCH RELIGION IS POISON!

*Compulsive salvation.* Some parents are so intent on saving the souls of their children that they create a religious phobia in them. The children are overwhelmed by religion administered in huge bad-tasting doses. When they grow old enough to rebel, they may disown all of the desirable stabilizing influences of religion too.

*Oppressive guilt.* Succumbing to temptation, failing to fulfill vows to God, indulging in sin; unable to forgive themselves, some people punish themselves daily for the rest of their lives.

*Only ones.* Some people convince themselves that theirs is the only true religion, and that it is their duty to either (1) keep themselves and their children from associating with (and thus becoming contaminated by) "lovers of the devil"—that is, most ordinary people or (2) go out and save the heathen by force. The Puritans were strong on witch burning and passing blue laws to force people to be good.

*Religious debates.* This exciting sport can shatter a believer's faith. A simple, contented faith is a healthy thing; well-informed confusion is not. You see, a debater's purpose is to disprove and discredit his opponent's data.

*Mixed marriages.* When each marriage partner's religious faith is so strong that he's convinced that he is right and the other wrong, then all sorts of emotional problems show up. Relatives are very cool to an "outsider." It is tough on children to decide which is right, whether to accept both denominations equally, and if so how to take the parents' emotional convictions seriously.

*Traditional folklore.* A large amount of the religious impressions picked up by children must be unlearned in their teens. Sunday-school lessons, words of hymns, scripture memory verses, bits of sermons, may create mental-image pictures which don't make good sense. When children discover that some of their articles of faith are as fictitious as Humpty Dumpty and the Easter bunny, their world is shaken! They are chagrined that they were suckered into believing and trusting. From now on they will be doubtful and suspicious.

Comparative religion college courses and religious radio stations create two problems which tend to erode a working faith. (1) They saturate the mind, overwhelm the senses. Too much of anything effectively reduces its value. (2) Analyzing the meaningful content of dozens of radio sermons and trying to grasp the authoritative theme in each of a dozen world religions becomes formidable. It is a religious jungle. There are a few beaten paths, but do they go anywhere except to quaint little native villages (denominations, cults)?

## NO RELIGION

*Agnosticism.* The theory that many cannot know the real truth, but only personal impressions which cannot be proved.

*Atheism.* The denial of God's existence, of all spirit beings; therefore the Bible and other authoritative religious teachings are invalid and foolish.

*Skepticism.* The method of critical examination and of suspending judgment on all philosophical and religious questions. A doubting or incredulous state of mind.

If too much religion is like a jungle of tangled ideas, no religion is like a desert. Hopefully, we will find a way to sift out meaningful truths so that we can have the advantages of a personal faith to live by without being overwhelmed by what seems to us to be mystical nonsense. Perhaps it is each man for himself. Most people agree that the greatest good and the least harm comes from voluntary participation in religious activities and studies.

The Constitution of the United States guarantees freedom of religion. A person can belong to any sect, cult or denomination he chooses—*or none at all!* Millions of people have selected the none-at-all attitude. They have been overwhelmed by the freedom of all religions to preach their "mystical nonsense." Finally they say to themselves, "To hell with the whole business!"

Emotional First Aid teaches that people should have some, but not too much, religion. Each person should have some because (1) some moral codes have merit, (2) churches are usually good social centers, (3) our culture is steeped in religious history and symbolism, and to deny it and reject or fight it places a person in a "can't belong, can't have" position. Parents who denounce religion may deny their children a free choice and access to an important part of our culture.

Suppose the agnostics are right: "Truth is not absolute, but only relative. People must select what is *meaningful for them.*"

Let's give the skeptics credit for honest, critical examination and assume that they are willing to recognize a good idea. Most skeptics can conscientiously accept a *general* statement. What is intolerable to them is a final, authoritative, absolute, this-is-it blanket statement.

What can we concede to atheism? God is dead, you say? So what? Surely we have moral attitudes, psychological hypotheses and spiritual concepts which seem reasonable and serve society—which are here, now, God or no God. *No one can believe everything.* Each of us must weigh and accept what seems reasonable and useful, rejecting much.

The following three essays are intended to be general statements acceptable to skeptics as possible articles of faith. These points of view permit skeptics to join the faithful in meaningful speculation and thus avoid those corrosive theological debates.

## AN ENGINEER'S PROOF OF GOD

Engineers are skeptical. No mysteries and dogmas for them. Give them data they can put into a formula or chart on a graph. Being able to discuss an idea with numbers seems to make that idea real no matter how fantastic it is. (New fantastic ideas with numbers: a thousand light-years away; giga-hertz [billion cycles per second]; nano-second [one billionth of a second]; megaton; micron; etc.)

One definition of "God": infinite awareness (omnipresent), infinite ability (omnipotent), infinite wisdom (omniscient). Mock up a gradient scale of awareness, ability and wisdom. Postulate infinite perfection at the top and a basic unit of one at the bottom. Enter typical (average) values for several finite circumstances. Connect the points with a line to form a graph. Additional values may be extrapolated (assume that the trend holds true for larger numbers).

You're right. The chart doesn't prove anything actually. It is a thinking tool capable of explaining the idea of expanding awareness and ability. To a dog the understanding of a child is infinitely great. A twelve-year-old boy cannot possibly comprehend the interest and insights of his college-professor father. Perhaps it is enough for skeptics to finally agree that there could be other intellectual realities than their own, both smaller and larger.

Another engineer's proof: logical deduction from existing evidence. Engineers know that it takes a lot of understanding, planning and skill to design, collect materials, assemble and tune up a car or a TV set. You don't just shake bits of iron, copper and glass together in a big basket. Who makes the flowers, kittens and babies? We don't know, but something does.

Scientists don't hesitate to use $x$ for an unknown something that must be there because they can see what it is doing.

## WHAT DOES A GOOD CHURCH DO?

So you have decided to support a church for the good of your children and your community. Which one? There may be a dozen denominations in your neighborhood. Is one just as good as another? Here are a few ideas to suggest contributions that a church can make to you, your family and your community.

*Appreciation and convictions.* Teach the children, and remind the adults, of the wonders of Creation and the satisfactions of a good life. Teach the Christian heritage and the history of the church. Help everyone to adopt high moral standards and to

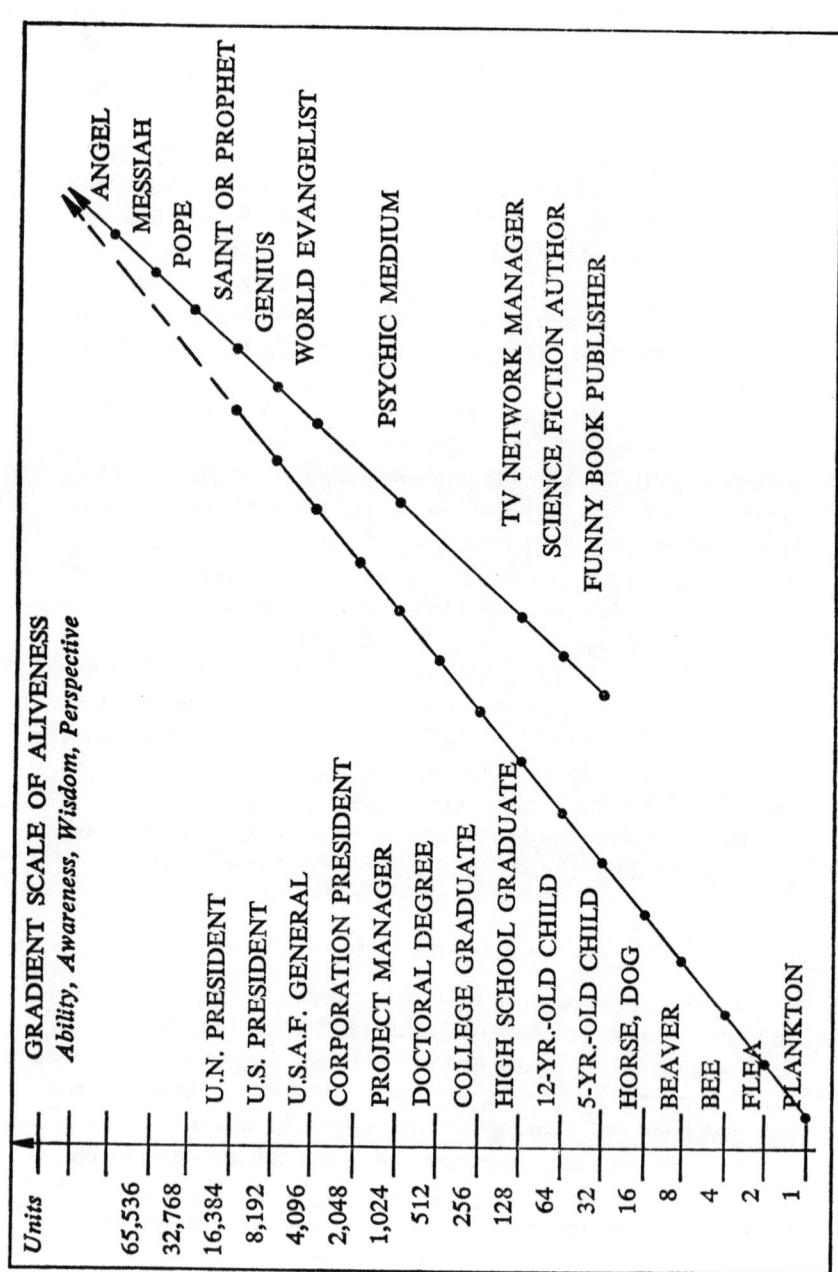

develop inner resources of purposeful convictions and courage. Clean, responsible citizenship is still worthwhile.

*Data source.* The church should provide sufficient data to young people so that they can make correct decisions without having to learn the hard way. They should have enough information on such things as sex, drinking, gambling, hypnosis, modern drugs, civil laws regarding marriage, population explosion, the economics of homemaking, applied psychology and mental health. We look to the church for some sort of compatible answers to deep spiritual and philosophical questions—the so-called mysteries of life. Young adults should not have to unlearn the early religious teachings which in some churches amount to weird folklore. There should be deliberate training in good citizenship. People need data when making decisions; innocence and ignorance are moral vacuums that suck in accidents and painful blunders.

*Applied psychology.* The church could make a fine contribution in the field of personality development by examining the poor communication, lack of moral thinking tools, and puny goals in our personal and business life. We all need coaching in positive thinking, establishing a healthy self-image and deliberately checking our intentions. People just naturally turn to their church for inspiration to be their very best and for the drive to keep on growing.

*Personal counseling.* We traditionally turn to our pastor for comfort when we are sick or bereaved. A church could provide Emotional First Aid, along the lines of Red Cross First Aid. Such a course would teach the danger signs of emotional disturbances and of the causes and remedies of mental strain and clearly state which conditions require immediate expert professional care. A really able Christian should be carefully trained to help others in many ways, including skills for effective lay counseling.

*Spiritual research.* (Wishful thinking here.) There should be a class for advanced spiritual students, a class for those who eagerly seek personal spiritual experience. This class would research and teach natural spiritual laws that really work—pushing back the spiritual frontier in the space age.

*Recreation.* It is natural to turn to the church for wholesome *family* recreation. This is a place to make new friends, to enjoy eating, singing and studying together, to meet the kind of people you like to know. Some churches sponsor scouts, drama clubs and orchestras.

*Opportunity to worship.* Though man has devised modern schemes for inspiring, comforting and guiding people, religious worship services are still wondrous and effective for many. Few people actually achieve a satisfying personal relationship with God, such as "salvation," "being born again" or "receiving a spiritual gift," but some do.

Many people who are turned off by theological debates on sin, hell and pearly gates might be able to stop resisting their religious friends and neighbors if they would refocus their attention on the church's other teachings mentioned above.

## EVERYBODY NEEDS A FAITH TO LIVE BY

Most adults agree to disagree about religion. There are too many denominations, too many authoritative contradictions. Which is right? Or are they all confused? Does it make any difference anyhow?

Call it character or conscience or personality, it is obvious that some people have pleasing friendly ways, an inner drive or purpose to get things done and the guts to see them through when the going is rough. What can we learn from such people, and how can we teach these traits to our children?

A judge was speaking to a group of parents and teachers. "Every day in my business I must talk to young people who have been caught breaking the law and causing trouble for themselves and society. They were arrested for being bad. I am supposed to convince them that they must be good in order to stay out of trouble. Parents and teachers, I ask you: What can a judge tell a child about being good in five minutes? Tell me what you are teaching your children about being good."

A fourth-grader remarked at the supper table one night, "The kids were talking about God and church this afternoon. Linda is a Catholic. Sue is a Methodist. Jane and Betty are J.W.'s. Daddy,

# Religion

what do we believe?" This father, an engineer by profession, was obviously not religious in any orthodox sense, or his daughter would certainly have known by age ten about the family's religious position. "Do we believe in the Trinity, salvation by the blood, the virgin birth and resurrection day?"

"No-o-o," the father replied thoughtfully, "but we certainly do have some other important beliefs." Then he thought up this list:

## THIS I BELIEVE

1. It *does* matter what I believe. There are important facts of life worth knowing. Good living requires realistic values, goals and perspectives.

2. It *does* matter what I read, whom I associate with and what I do with my free time. The real me reflects my environment. It is natural for me to tend to become like the people I live, work, study and play with.

3. A healthy body is always desirable and important. Everyone should learn about cleanliness, nutrition, safety and First Aid. Good living is impossible without a healthy body.

4. I believe that I should always do my part and do my best. I want to earn my way, and whenever possible contribute to the welfare and happiness of others. I will earn the love and respect of other people by my thoughtfulness and diligence.

5. I will always *care* about something and someone. I will try to be especially interested in a certain type of work, a special hobby, and love at least one person. I will never tell myself that nobody cares, or that nothing matters.

6. I will try to be friendly and courteous. I want people to trust me and be happy that I am with them; therefore I will cause no unnecessary pain or confusion. I will try to help others to be their best selves.

7. I will practice *moderation* with *judgment*. I will try to discern values and differences. I will try to estimate probable results from my actions so that I can accept responsibility for them.

8. I will try to find *courage* to make painful but proper decisions. Strength of character comes from doing what is best in the

long run, even if it hurts. I will face danger if necessary and fight if the cause is worth it.

9. I will protect my good name and especially my self-respect. I will live up to my own standards. If I do my best at all times, then others will care and will value my worth.

10. Guilt is a powerful evil force. It is usually possible to ask forgiveness, make amends and start afresh.

11. Fear is a powerful evil force. Sometimes we fear the unknown when in fact it may not be fearful at all. Listing the basic known facts may relieve anxiety and furnish new clues. I should not hesitate to ask for help in real emergencies.

12. Concepts of *good* and *bad* are best weighed on a gradient scale. Few actions and ideas are either black or white. Most have shades of gray which can best be understood by comparison with similar actions and ideas.

13. Spiritual gifts really do exist. A few people can foretell, do real faith healing, divine objects, and so on. People should learn about ESP and the powers of the mind so that they can sort out hoaxes and fairy tales from real psychic phenomena.

14. I should use my natural talents—*use them*. I should try to be a champ, not at everything but at something.

15. I should try to understand the other person's point of view before judging. If I knew what he knows and felt as he feels, then I would agree with him.

16. Any faith is better than none at all; therefore I should not scoff at the religious beliefs of others. It is usually possible to offer new useful ideas which do not conflict with their faith.

*That first group was sort of spiritual. This next group is perhaps more psychological, and more directly related to Emotional First Aid.*

17. Life is like a game. I will play to win but be willing to lose. I will learn the rules and play fair. I will try to help others have a good game, too.

18. I will practice thrift in all things: time, money, food, etc. This will help me accumulate reserve resources for emergencies and help me to care for and value my environment. Wasting is a form of dishonesty.

## Religion

19. I will always have a personal goal or plan for my future. I will think about it and picture it in my mind. I will visualize how happy I will be when my dream comes true. Every fine thing was in someone's imagination before it became real.

20. Good habits are tools to get things done when there is not time to think. They will protect me from danger. They are my social graces and my personality.

21. I should have a personal Emotional First Aid procedure. I should plan what I should do in the event of a great loss or disappointment or the death of a loved one or other great emotional shock.

22. Everyone has emotional cycles, or moods. I should understand them, guarding against the lows and making the most of the highs. I should learn ways to be at my best more often.

23. We all have psychological pushbuttons—certain things we do automatically: phobias, allergies, quirks, compulsions. It helps to understand that people sometimes do foolish things because they simply have to. This makes forgiveness easier.

24. It is important to finish what I start. Tiredness and failure come from leaving things undone. I will avoid starting things that can't be completed. I should help others finish their projects.

25. I should expect to be happy in my daily work—or find the reason why.

26. That which I can visualize I can have, or do. The first requirement of success is a good clear mental-image picture. I should try to avoid thinking about undesirable pictures.

27. I will remember that for every problem there is some sort of answer; that even in a disaster something sensible can be done to prevent further damage and suffering. Where there is still life, there should still be hope.

## SPIRITUAL GOALS

This is a list of spiritual goals some people have set for themselves.

1. To be happy most of the time and be able to bring some sunshine into the lives of those around me.

2. To take control of my environment: do the things I should do; be able to own some nice things; enjoy financial security; be proud of my career. (This is in contrast to "adjusting to one's environment" as recommended by some psychologists.)

3. To enjoy perfect physical health; heal cuts quickly; avoid accidents; feel fine and ready to go every day.

4. To be a symbol of good judgment and serenity in my community, so that those in trouble or confusion confidently seek me out for inspiration and counseling.

5. To have the inner feeling of abundance, so that I can gladly contribute to every project and every person I meet: to one, a word of praise; to another, a new point of view; here some technical data on a hobby, there a helping hand for a few minutes or hours.

6. To have an inner sense of right and wrong based on a firm knowledge of natural law, and the courage to confidently do right even when it seems to hurt.

7. To have enough insight into, and understanding of, human nature to be able to appreciate the compulsions and rationalizations of those about me—and my own.

8. To be the sort of person who inspires each of my friends to be his best self.

9. To cast a frequent glance at some "shining light" that is out in front and a little above—to keep myself growing.

## SUMMARY

1. Religion can be a powerful force for emotional health and stability. It can also cause fear, guilt, corrosive bickering and confusing dilemmas. There is a pronounced gradient scale of religious beliefs. (See following chart.)

2. A church is a natural moral authority in a community (at least for some people).

3. A church is a natural family social center.

4. A church is a natural Emotional First Aid center. People easily seek comfort and guidance from a pastor or priest.

5. One goal of Emotional First Aid is to achieve a happy medium between bigoted ignorance and extreme intellectual broad-mindedness. Two other extremes to be avoided: the militant skeptic intent on shattering the beliefs of the faithful, and the overzealous crusading soul-saver. However sincere and legitimate these extremists may be, their efforts undermine the good which can come from an optimum religious faith.

6. What is optimum?
—*Voluntary* interest.
—Satisfying participation in a local religious organization.
—A set of articles of faith *meaningful* to the individual.
—A minimum of unanswered theological riddles.

7. Emotional First Aid should utilize religion in these ways:
—Recommend that churches standardize a moral code for all of society.
—Advocate Emotional First Aid classes in churches.
—Utilize church custom and authority to sponsor lay counseling.
—Recommend a more meaningful gradient in religious teachings. (Lessons on morality and church dogma should emphasize points of easy logical agreement, limiting theological mysteries to selected advanced classes.)

## PREVENTION OF RELIGIOUS EMOTIONAL PROBLEMS

—Try to avoid teaching traditional folklore and symbolism which must be unlearned or apologized for when the child grows up.
—Avoid debates by conflicting authorities.
—Do not force religious ideas, studies, discussions or attendance. These should be voluntary.

—Acknowledge spiritual reality and parapsychology as possibilities.

—Discourage the constitutional right to hold no faith at all: this is a weak, irresponsible, unmoral position.

### GRADIENT SCALE OF RELIGIOUS ATTITUDES

| Dedicated, Obsessed | Active Members | No Interest | Debaters, Church jumpers | Persecutors, Denouncers, Religious War |
|---|---|---|---|---|
| Nun | Tither | | Neurotics | Crusaders |
| Monk | Memorizer | "Send | Skeptics | Communists |
| Missionary | Church worker | the | Relig. professors | |
| Prophet | | kids" | | Fascists |
| Saint | | | Christmas | Fanatics |
| Messiah | "Only ones" | | Easter | |
| | Cultist | | Funerals only | |

## CHAPTER 15

# *Time*

"Time" can be thought of as:
—Apparency of change, rate of change, speed.
—Sense of continuity, continuous existence.
—Period allotted to some specific purpose: length of service, sentence, course, event.
—Schedule to start/regulate/stop a series of events in a proper sequence.
—Synchronize concurrent events in phase.
—Cycles.
—Perspective of past, present and future times.
—Sense of values is related to time.

## SOME EMOTIONAL PROBLEMS INVOLVING TIME

—Boredom: the feeling of tremendous anxiety when interesting events occur too slowly.
—Confusion, frustration: anxiety, discouragement, loss of perspective when events occur too fast.
—Painful loss: sensing a loss *suddenly*.
—Fearful panic: being threatened *suddenly*.
—Slow thinking, slow reading and problem solving, because of poor training and bad habits.
—Habitual tardiness, procrastination; lack of perseverance.
—Inability to sense, or feel, time periods and relationships in order to make long-term plans, or to judge costs and values by estimating time requirements.
—Compulsive psychological cycles, moods, somatics, etc.

Some students complain that school is a bore; so they drop out. Most dropouts will spend the rest of their lives in boring poverty, working at unskilled jobs such as ditch digger, parts assembler, security guard, janitor. Students who conquer boredom and finish school have earned a wide variety of occupations and may be permitted to change jobs whenever they wish.

Much mischief and vandalism is explained by "We were bored. There wasn't anything else to do." Some wives feel justified in getting a divorce because of boredom. "He doesn't need me any more. I don't know what to do with myself."

Some homes have a nightly harangue about getting the kids to bed. They know they are going to bed soon, but not "now." Parents have to tease and threaten, thus creating for themselves the role of cruel dictator. They perpetuate the illusion that it is permissible to have an emotional confrontation every night at bedtime. Perhaps this is a childish scheme for getting a little attention, a scheme that works so well it may become a lifelong habit to procrastinate.

One kind of finance company helps you to get out of debt. It charges a fee to mail your money to your creditors. You honestly intended to pay them sometime but not now. Your procrastination has cost you extra money, your credit rating and lots of worry.

Some people are habitually unemployed because they can't sense time. What can you do with a man who is usually late arriving at work? The rest of the gang is ready to start, but Joe didn't show. He just let himself roll over and go back to sleep. Then there is the type who is usually on time, works hard, learns easily, gets along well, but occasionally disappears. He doesn't come to work for a few days. Perhaps he gets drunk or goes hunting or goes cross country to see his mother. His sense of future time is very short. It is as if there were a big white sheet hanging in tomorrow so that he can't see the next day or next week. He has no concern about how to explain to the boss where he has been, or the possibility of getting fired again.

Perhaps this is why some students quit school; they can't see any future in it. (Review Psycho-cybernetics, chap. 12.)

## GRADIENT SCALE OF TIME SENSE

—"Saves" time; skillful in arts and sports, plans well.
—Always on time; prompt, reliable, patient, busy.

# Time

—Usually on time; usually reliable, on schedule.
—Usually a little late; plans for future usually indefinite.
—Always late; impatient, impetuous; procrastinates.
—May forget to come at all; no plans or dreams for future.
—Timeless apathy; nothing matters, nothing is interesting.

Boredom is a painful emotion to many people. Boredom may cause a person to do something—*anything*—to create some action: make noises, get into mischief, carve designs in furniture with a penknife. Some people feel compelled to have a radio going all of the time, no matter what the program or the clarity of the sound, just so long as something is happening. They have the habit. Withdrawal symptoms begin to show when comparative silence and serenity set in. For them, solitary confinement would be an unbearable torture. Strangely, a "fix" for people with the sound-motion habit may be as simple and meaningless as the "yea, yea, yea—beat, beat, beat" of a tiny radio, or playing solitaire.

## CYCLES

Our lives are full of biological, physiological and emotional cycles, of which much has already been published. Only a few special ideas are mentioned here.

*Unfinished cycles.* Quitting jobs or hobbies before a natural cycle is completed tends to make a person tired and listless. The habit of starting things and not finishing leads to frustration and impotence.

"Nice" people unknowingly inflict impotence on their children, friends and fellow workers by (1) helping people before they need or ask for help, (2) protecting people before they are hurt, (3) giving them a free ride—welfare, gravy-train jobs, snap courses. It has been said that it is wrong to help a chick crack its shell or to help a baby kangaroo creep into its mother's pouch the first time. They should complete the natural cycle *themselves*.

An unfinished cycle creates a hangup. Of course, there is a gradient scale of hangups. Some are very small and common, everyday affairs that go unnoticed, *but the subconscious keeps score.* They add up, like straws on a camel's back. Big hangups cause painful warping of personalities. One of the rules in psychoanalysis: "Look for the unfinished cycle."

*Emotional-cycle delay factor.* An emotional *effect* may or may not follow the *cause* immediately. The effect may not occur for minutes, hours or days after an emotional shock. (See chap. 9 on Emotional Shock.) Having an extended delay between cause and effect is critically important when teaching safety, prevention, responsibility, and law and justice to people. About half the population is below "average" and have some impairment in their time sense. For them rules, laws and dogma probably serve better than hoping to rely on their common sense and logic. A child learns about hot stoves easily because pain follows burn instantly. Learning about infection from a cut, good care of teeth, venereal disease and pregnancy is slower and less certain because of the delay between cause and effect. Learning respect for the law is slow and uncertain when people must wait from six months to over a year for a trial.

*Com lag.* A communication lag is that period of time between receiving an incoming communication or signal and the moment an appropriate reply or response is made. In high-speed sports the champions must make their moves in fractions of a second. Decisions must be made in split seconds when driving in five-o'clock traffic. When you tell a six-year-old child to go to bed, you don't mind a one-minute delay, but a ten-minute delay is too much. If you mail an order to Sears or Wards, waiting for your package seven days seems reasonable; if it hasn't come in three weeks, you become irritated. Workers have been known to write up suggestions and put them in the suggestion box, then wait for their award. Nothing happens. Weeks go by. Not even an acknowledgment is received: "Your suggestion is under consideration." Workers have been known to get very upset by such long unexplained com lags. Some even quit if their boss takes too long to answer them. Another dandy is, "I was promised a raise five weeks ago. Why haven't I got it yet?"

## PREVENTING EMOTIONAL TIME PROBLEMS

1. Try to keep a normal schedule; avoid sudden changes, but if changes are necessary, bridge into them as gently as possible, and explain why. Maintain continuity.

2. Teach children about time: (1) importance of promptness, (2) planning ahead, (3) doing things now, (4) enduring, even enjoying quiet times, or simple keep-busy ways to avoid boredom.

3. Try to finish things once started, or at least reach a good stopping place, so that a sub-cycle will be ended.

4. Don't interrupt other people's cycles by helping too much. Usually they should do their own thing even if it fails.

5. Don't expect too much of people with short-time senses. They may fail at simple tasks because they are literally lost in time.

6. Don't spread yourself too thin, that is, try to do more than you have time for. Some people run, run, run from one errand or meeting to another, all day long, every day. Some very able people schedule naps for themselves every day. These little time islands seem to help them be at their best more often. Naps tend to help end cycles too.

7. If you are a clock watcher, the chances are you don't enjoy your job. Do you wish your life away? Wish for five o'clock to hurry around, wish for payday, wish for a holiday, wish for bowling night? If your "right now" is so dull, you should start planning for a change.

## CHAPTER 16

# Love

It has been said, "To love is to be hurt." This quotation hints at the painful sense of loss experienced when love stops, whether terminated by the death of a loved one, long separation such as required by military duties, or divorce.

There are many kinds of love:
—Self-love, egoism, self-centeredness.
—Love for a mate, feeling of oneness, desire for intimacy.
—Love for one's family, tribe, country, alma mater, group.
—Love for animals, flowers, other living things.
—Love for science, physics, mechanics, electronics.
—Love for spirit entities, spiritual and psychic studies.
—Love for God and His special prophets and manifestations.

Here are some common expressions to illustrate that the word love is vague, almost an unknown:
—"God is love."
—"Love thy neighbor as thyself."
—"Make love to me."
—"That dog loves his master."
—"Love is the opposite of hate, and so if you don't hate someone, you must love him." (One person's explanation of how she could love everybody.)

Bodies have a physical attraction for each other, besides the desire for sex. People and animals like to be close to, and touch, those they trust and admire. They like to rub, fondle, pet, caress, wrestle, eat and sleep with, work and play with, each other. This devotion can become so strong that a lover may risk his life for his beloved. Man for man, dog for man, mother for child. What is this power?

People can love a great leader. Some love his courage and thoughtfulness in caring for them. Some admire his skill and resourcefulness. Some appreciate his fine contribution to their welfare and security; they are thankful and grateful. Some see in him a standard of excellence, an ideal, a hero. Some admire his superior strength, cunning, wisdom and ability to mete out justice. Other leaders love him because he is one of them; they can communicate man to man.

After their bodies' physical hunger for sex is satisfied, a man and woman can love each other for several reasons. Each has a thirst for intimate communication. Each of us needs to belong to someone, to know that someone cares about what we think and do. We need a good terminal: to show off to, to fight for, to be inspired by, to need us, to share our victories and losses.

A lover gives meaning to our lives and their daily activities. A lover is a reference for establishing values—all kinds of values: economic, moral, interpersonal, spiritual. On the eve of divorce, when it becomes evident that love has gone and one is all alone, many a person has felt the devastating shatter of his values. All that he stood for, all that he has earned and built suddenly become valueless.

Real love can sometimes be built on imagination. It is often true that love is blind, and the young man and young woman fall in love with the symbolic mask of loveliness each subconsciously puts over the other's head. This is easily done, since each is on his best behavior during courting. Each indulges in wishful thinking, having long dreamed of an ideal mate, and longed for the time of intimacy to come.

Real love? Is there any other kind? Isn't puppy love real? Short-termed perhaps; ill-advised, awkward, inopportune perhaps; but burning, purposeful, inspiring, blinding, bringing delightful and painful sensations, values, meaning. I say, "If it grabs ya, it's real." I can add, "If it dumps ya, it was real."

" 'Tis better to have loved and lost than never to have loved at all." From one point of view loving is a fine game. Not to love at all is missing a lot of fun. More important, it is dangerous. Being unloved seems to prove, "Nobody cares. Nothing matters. I am nobody." These are sick ideas. *Everybody* should love *somebody;* loneliness is a very serious disability.

In her poem "Why Do I Love Thee?" Elizabeth Barrett Browning wrote, "I love you, not for what you are, but for what I am when I am with you." Love makes us want to be at our best, not just for our beloved but for the whole world. A wonderful girl can make her man feel ten feet tall.

Love at first sight? Soul mates? Some couples experience exciting pleasant sensations and radiant warmth at their first meeting. Though incredible, it almost seems that they are long-lost lovers reunited, and their cup runneth over. No preliminary courting seems necessary, no checking of credentials, no exploratory communications, no questions. How can we explain that feeling which seems to sing, "I'm home at last, safely in your arms where I belong"?

## ARC—A NEW WORD FOR LOVE

Industrial psychologists and human engineers can't bring themselves to speak of love. It doesn't seem dignified to say that management is making love to the union or that the troops love their sergeant. Furthermore, the word "love" is too vague to be scientific; it means too many different things to people. What was needed, the engineers decided, was a word for love that doesn't mean emotion and sex. Cut out the emotion! And cut out the fun play! Who'd want what's left?

Like splitting the atom, they split "love" and found that it has three parts: Affinity, Reality and Communication. Next they did a sort of spectrum analysis on each of these; they put them on a gradient scale.

Here are dictionary definitions: *Affinity*—spontaneous attraction to or liking for; closeness, tied together; friendly connection; attracting force, the desire or tendency to unite; togetherness. *Reality*—truth, actuality; objective existence in fact; a clear, easily understood conception; accurate representation; sensible, believable; fidelity to nature. *Communication*—giving and receiving ideas or objects; an interpersonal exchange. [See chap. 5 on Communication and chap. 13 on Stable Data and Meaningful Truth.]

# Love

ARC is the common denominator in all interpersonal relationships. The ARC factors may be high or low, good or bad, but they are ever-present. Here is a simple gradient scale illustrating their relationships.

| Affinity | Reality | Communication |
|---|---|---|
| Intimate devotion, very close | Complete agreement; precise accuracy | Intuitive, fast, accurate; intimate, confidential |
| Affectionate; high regard | Usually agree; rational difference | Usually good for practical purposes |
| Acquaintance | Presumed reasonable | Limited, cautious, courteous routines |
| Respected enemy | Enforced; legalistic | Only as required |
| Open anger, hate | Exaggerated, lies | Fierce, loud |
| "I'll kill you!" | Unreasonable | No talk, just force |
| Fear: "I'm dangerous" or "Protect me" | Interested only in offense or defense | Compulsive, intermittent, incomplete |
| Grief: "Poor me" or "You poor thing" | Interested only in sad things, losses | Little attempt to communicate at all |
| Apathy: "I don't know and I don't care" | Things are hazy Nothing seems real | Garbled, incoherent; babble, silence |

High affinity means, "I like you"; "You have credit with me good for favors and personal services whenever you ask." (See "Brownie Points," p. 51.)

High reality means making sense and being on the level.

Communication, as it turned out, is much more vital to man's welfare and happiness than love is. You could, I suppose, live a whole lifetime without ever being in love—and even despise yourself. But to live without communicating is almost unthinkable. Certainly it would be a shorter and lonelier life. Seeing that communication is so important, the human engineers busied themselves splitting it for further analysis and found fourteen basic parts. A good communication consists of:

—Sender.
—Receiver.
—Particle: the message, package, candy, bullet, etc.
—Mass of the particle: its size and weight.
—Velocity of the particle: how fast it is traveling.
—Distance—between sender and receiver.
—Intention of sender: how eager or accurate he is.
—Attention of receiver: is he tuned in and listening/watching?
—Ability of the receiver to understand and value the message.
—Acknowledgment by receiver: "Message received okay."
—Distortion—changes, cracks, bends, twists.
—Interference—noise, static, adulteration, pollution.
—Attenuation—the particle gets smaller and weaker.
—Metacom—the invisible, subconscious meaning.
(See more details in chap. 5 on Communication.)

Low ARC between people causes all kinds of trouble. Usually the best way to clear trouble is to communicate some more. You can't expect to do business or solve problems if both parties go away mad and never see each other again. "When in doubt, communicate" is a good rule of thumb for solving emotional problems. Have you noticed that there is a natural tendency to stop communicating when ARC is low, which can only make matters worse? If you find ways to keep the receiver party saying, "Yes, yes," then affinity must go up. Whatever makes one of the ARC factors go down depresses them all; whatever makes one of the factors go up raises them all.

## SOME EMOTIONAL PROBLEMS INVOLVING LOVE

1. Loneliness. "Everybody needs somebody."
2. Passion. The instinctive mating drive that eagerly reaches out with intense emotion, an irresistible impulse tending toward physical indulgence.

# Love

3. Sudden loss. Death, divorce, competition, illness, prison.
4. Betrayal. Divorce, infidelity, cheating about money.
5. One-way love (see chap. 22 on Family Counseling).
6. Emotional hangups. Frigidity, marrying a symbolic father image or mother image; marrying for security or for pride of possession; marrying on the rebound after being jilted. Getting married in order to leave an oppressive home or in order to get plenty of sex legally.
7. Learning how to "love" from examples of clumsy parents. Bad training.
8. Free love. Saturation, disillusionment, degraded perspective.
9. Legal problems. Responsibilities, community property.
10. Innocence. Unwanted pregnancy, V.D., shotgun weddings.
11. The Big Lie. "True love is forever" ("people don't change").
12. Photo magic. The lover places a mask over the beloved which hides his true identity and personality. She sees what she hopes to see—the image of the White Knight of her dreams.
13. Jealousy. Especially the big, sick kind.
14. Possessiveness. The compulsion to try to change a spouse.

## SOME WAYS TO PREVENT UNNECESSARY EMOTIONAL SUFFERING

1. Help lonely people to "find somebody."
2. Teach the "facts of life" about pregnancy, disease, laws.
3. Teach the difference between passion and well-established ARC.
4. Teach the principles of photo magic: select the sort of person you want to love *before* courting. It is often too late to use good judgment *after* love starts.
5. Personal counseling should be easily available and encouraged.
6. Don't seek love. Seek good ARC: respect, compatibility and good mutual games. (See chap. 4 on Games.) To be a good lover, be worthy of respect, be sincere (good reality) and learn to communicate skillfully.

7. Teach the truth about true love lasting forever. Love *can* fade if it is not nourished and tended. It can be poisoned and stamped out by being betrayed. And people can change: some mature faster than others. Some people develop emotional hang-ups and even serious psychological problems which make them unlovable. Being forewarned will not prevent such love casualties, but forewarning may at least help to reduce guilt and help people to observe dying loveships more intelligently.

8. Many people act as if they thought that love equals sex. They never experienced good ARC, and probably they don't know anyone who did. Surely we can create situations where boys and girls can experience good games together, feel admiration, respect and pride in good teamwork and share hopes and losses together. Remember, perhaps half of our homes operate on a cold-war basis. Good ARC is unknown to millions of people! "Average" is only halfway up the gradient scale. Half the people are below average, and that is bleak emotional training for the children in those families and schools!

9. Teach the importance of fair play. All is not fair in love and war. We know that war is a dirty business, but love doesn't have to be. Courtesy and decency can be taught. The golden rule should prevail.

10. Try to avoid puritanical moral judgment of others. All is not black and white in the areas of sex behavior, divorce, sex education and schemes for selecting mates.

11. Discuss sex and love frankly with children. Mystery and innocence invite accidents and stupid blunders. Secrecy is low ARC.

12. If love is the greatest thing in the world, as Drummond proved in his essay by that name, how is it we don't have classes?

# CHAPTER 17

# *Anger and Healthy Fights*

Anger is that intimacy which pushes people apart.

Anger is strong, violent displeasure, exasperation, indignation, fury, hatred, resentment, rage, wrath, impatience, temper, inflamed irritation, hostility.

Anger is an emotional response to a dilemma, to an unbearable situation. It indicates a strong interest, a vital concern. It is a reactionary emotion demanding a change.

Anger is extravagant, uncompromising, bent on destruction, shortsighted, seeks explosive force, exaggerates values of things and principles. It reduces general awareness, curtails logic, causes chronic withdrawal and isolation. It seeks to demolish, overthrow, cause ruin, utterly destroy, undermine, shake the foundation, overturn, extinguish, abolish.

Anger is hostile. It demands an enemy, an antagonist. It is malicious, warlike, destructive.

Anger is an emotion known to tense muscles and nerves, change body functions and chemistry. Chronic anger can contribute to indigestion, ulcers, constipation, arthritis, bad body odors and skin disorders.

Suppressed anger causes fear, covert hostility and subversiveness. Suppressed anger causes a will to fail, an inner compulsion to stop the game—dump the chess board, get a divorce, quit the job. It is such a powerful force for destruction that it warrants prompt skillful therapy.

Not all anger is necessarily bad. An emotionally mature person experiences anger over a specific situation which has caused righteous indignation. Anger turns him on, and he insists on getting things straightened out. After the situation is remedied, anger changes to a new higher level of ARC; the air is cleared after the storm. Here anger insists on communicating about the problem, and the person's mature habits and attitudes prevent unnecessary harm and destruction, thus preserving the basis for continuing respect and friendship after the matter is settled.

Much anger is immature, however. It doesn't concern a specific situation which can be remedied. There is no chance of clearing the air. It is a habitual, compulsive personality trait, just as some people have a loving personality. There is much unnecessary name calling and irreversible destruction. Much of the pressure and energy is suppressed into the subconscious, where it can cause untold antisocial mischief. One possible problem is the "substitute terminals" phenomenon which creates bullies. Not knowing what he is angry at, or with whom, the bully tries to have it out with anybody and everybody. Innocent people become victims of his inner rage and frustration. His physical condition displays plenty of psychosomatics. He is unhappy inside and out.

## EMOTIONAL PREVENTION REGARDING ANGER

1. Teach that anger is okay sometimes—if you can remedy a specific problem with it. Not *all* anger should be suppressed as bad.

2. Try to find a suitable scheme to express anger and resentment in some sort of dynamic cycle. Think of anger as energy that has to come out somehow or make you sick. Even chopping wood with all your might or scrubbing floors can help discharge that energy. Seeking expert emotional counseling is the best way, of course.

3. Appoint, sponsor, recommend, train, referees. A fair fight can do a lot of good. Having a referee raises the dignity of a fist fight or debate: the referee helps make the outcome certain and final.

4. Observe angry children to try to understand the real underlying cause. There are many possibilities, including malnutrition, aching teeth, poor eyes or ears, being in the wrong grade in school (see article in Aug., 1966, *Reader's Digest*). The child may be disturbed about his parents' fighting at home. It is possible that the real cause of his angry disposition can be remedied quite easily if you can find it.

## RULES FOR MAKING THE MOST OF ANGER\*

1. Acknowledge that you get angry. It's okay to get angry sometimes. Don't hide your anger and lie to yourself. Anger is energy and must be discharged somehow. Anger stored inside can cause problems, like "sick headache." Catharsis is good. Find safe ways to get anger out.

2. Don't run away from a partner's anger. Anger is asking for love, communication and understanding. A tantrum is a purposeful act to get attention. Expressed anger is an attempt to change behavior.

3. Listen, listen, listen. Ask, "What brings you to that conclusion?" Perception check: "I seem to hear you say . . ."

4. Avoid overwhelming your partner. Don't knock him down or try to outshout him.

5. Express your feelings. Be explicit. Be honest. Be accurate. It is permissible and safe to report your personal feelings. This gives your opponent needed data and does not require defensive action.

6. Don't hit below the belt. Fight fair. Dirty fighting results when you can't express frankly. Don't use uncomplimentary information received in friendly confidence as ammunition in a fight. Confucius say, "Man who call names admits he has run out of good ideas."

7. Don't be a grievance collector—that is, don't keep a little black book. Don't save up troubles; they seem to grow if kept warm. Don't confuse the present issue with old stuff. Being a martyr can prevent further communications of all kinds, including problem solving.

8. Attack the problem, not each other. You can't solve the problem if you don't work on it.

9. Don't handicap yourself by tackling the problem at a bad time (on an empty stomach, for instance).

10. Don't leave loose ends. End the fight definitely, if pos-

---
\* From notes on a lecture by Dr. M. Tikton, Sept., 1968.

sible; don't quit midway. Don't try to soften the action just when it gets going good. Finish it. End the cycle.

"Anger nearby affects me. Somehow it seems to imply that I'm to blame. It makes me nervous and defensive. It limits my communications." Fighting parents can really upset a child even though he only listens through a closed door.

We are healthy in personal relationships to the degree that we can express personal feelings. It is important to tell other people how we feel—often.

Suggested reading: George R. Bach and Peter Wyden, *The Intimate Enemy* (Wm. Morrow, pub.).

CHAPTER 18

# *Grief*

Grief is sorrow caused by a great loss from death or disaster. Grief is emotional suffering, mourning, loneliness.

Grief is associated with affliction, injustice, distress, agony, melancholy, tribulation, oppressive sense of being wronged, atrocious destruction, depression of spirit, gloom, dejection, despondency, great disappointment.

Most people must eventually face the death of grandparents, then parents and other beloved relatives and finally their spouses. Many homes must confront the loss or serious injury of a man in military service. Auto accidents claim thousands. Hundreds of thousands of homes are dismembered by divorce. Such incidents create emotional shock, with its characteristic loss of awareness and sense of responsibility. (See chap. 9 on Emotional Shock.) People in grief should be given the full treatment for shock to prevent unnecessary additional suffering. Decisions concerning money and property should be avoided while under the influence of grief; they seem trivial compared to the loss of a loved one. Foolish costly decisions are sometimes made while people are overwhelmed with emotion.

Perhaps the most harm can come from being "brave" and avoiding proper grieving. It is natural to feel grief; even animals do. Avoiding a funeral or deliberately doing something else to take your mind off the death of a loved one is emotionally dangerous. Suppressing a powerful emotion such as grief or anger stores it in the subconscious, where it may bubble and boil and cause hangups for the rest of a lifetime. If grief is there, it must be experienced, confronted and run out sooner or later, and the sooner the better. Fresh grief is easily found and identified and easily discharged as compared to laborious psychotherapy, which may require searching the subconscious for particular incidents among hundreds down through the years. Facing up to fresh grief is a little like cleaning and dressing a wound in order to prevent festering and poisoning later.

People in grief are low-toned. They lose their stable data, are reluctant to communicate. Everyday affairs seem far away and unimportant; they are careless about their physical health, eating, sleeping, and so on. Games? It seems cruel to mention games to a grief-stricken person. Interest in the community, national or world affairs? None. Their havingness is shot. Self-image is limited to "poor me." Time is unreal. Religion is limited to "After death, what?" It is easy for a mourning wife or husband to consider suicide. Life without the loved one promises to be bleak, hopeless and meaningless.

## HOW TO FACE GRIEF

It was discovered that the tearful loss of self-control comes in waves or cycles, somewhat similar to seasickness. When the beautiful sadness causes uncontrolled sobbing, don't try to turn it off. Cry. If certain phrases seem to trigger the waves of emotion, repeat them to yourself. "He's gone forever." "I'll never see him again." "He was such a good, kind man." "Now I'm alone." "I didn't even know he was suffering." "We had such a beautiful life together." Perhaps looking at his picture or his favorite chair or listening to his favorite record will turn you on. That's all right. Turn on and get it over with; then you will have a few minutes of relief before the next surge of sorrow. After a while the periods will become hours apart, then days apart. As the weeks turn to months you will be able to recall the wonderful memories you have of the loved one free of compulsive sadness.

People who suppress their grief risk becoming neurotic or psychotic. Some may break into tears years after the funeral. Some may find ways to blank out their finest memories: they may avoid all social life and become hermits; they may make rash promises, such as "I'll never laugh again" or "I'll never love again." There are many ways to get hung up over suppressed grief, and many of them are not so obvious as crying. Emotions which are suppressed into the subconscious may become the basic cause of psychosomatic ills, weird moods or perhaps phobias. Grief is very low on the gradient scale. People who are stuck in grief just naturally attract many other low-scale manifestations. (See the gradient scale in chap. 3. Chronic grief is below fear and just barely above complete apathy.)

## EMOTIONAL FIRST AID FOR A GRIEF-STRICKEN PERSON

1. Assume guard position. Treat the person for shock. Don't let him wander into danger or do something foolish.

2. Notify authorities and relatives if necessary.

3. More care for children, pets, furnace, farm animals, etc.

4. Encourage dignified weeping and mourning. Ward off well-meaning relatives who try to cheer him up and "take his mind off it." Keep the use of alcohol and tranquilizers to a minimum.

5. Offer bits of appropriate philosophy tactfully. A good idea can be a lifesaver at a time when everything seems hopeless.

6. Just be there. When everything else is done, *don't go*. Never leave a person who is in shock alone.

7. Don't lie to a child about death or divorce. Don't force him to confront more than he seems to need to, but on the other hand don't shut him out of vital situations. He needs to know basic facts. His grief and suffering may be rather casual—or deep and bitter. If he is very upset, help him express it, feel it and run it out; don't let him avoid confronting the situation, thus suppressing it into his subconscious, where it may cause trouble for a lifetime.

8. For yourself: when grief comes to you: (1) Admit that you are in shock and thus emotionally disabled: (2) Review in your mind the basic do's and don't's for a person in shock. Try to help yourself. (3) Accept help from someone. If there is no close friend or relative you can call on, it might be wise to hire an aide for a few days, perhaps a housekeeper, nurse or secretary, or perhaps a student social worker or student pastor. (4) Avoid making important decisions about money and property;

if a decision must be made, seek professional advice first. (5) Face your grief courageously and cry it out. Don't bug out with booze or drugs. Don't try to avoid your grieving by working extra hard.

## CAN WE PREPARE FOR A CRISIS?

1. Some events are predictable. Death from old age, for instance, seldom happens unexpectedly. The flooding of a valley can be expected following heavy snows and a week of warm rain. Forewarning is forearming for people who have the courage to face the facts.

2. Some situations have a high risk. Commercial insurance policies can help soften an otherwise disastrous calamity.

3. Exchanging lists of household goods with relatives could be important. A list made from memory for the fire-insurance company after a house burns down may be incomplete.

4. Does your personal phone book have a list of the numbers to call for doctor, police, firemen, next-door neighbors, close relatives and friends so that every member of your family can find them instantly? Sometimes minutes count.

5. Some old folks save their loved ones considerable anguish by preplanning their funeral arrangements. "When my time comes, just call this number. I've told the funeral director just what I want done."

6. Much unnecessary suffering is caused by the absence of a will. Another frightful situation is the lack of cash after a husband's death. There may be no income for weeks or months while a perfectly proper will goes through legal red tape.

7. Do you have enough cash or credit to enable you to dash across the country to be at a parent's bedside? You should plan to go if possible, in spite of the trouble and expense. You may feel guilty for the rest of your life if you don't.

8. Help others. In so doing you will learn Emotional First Aid facts before you need them for yourself. You can soften your own suffering when it comes if you become somewhat familiar with such matters secondhand.

*Grief*

9. Make a list of your insurance policies, bank accounts, business connections and relatives. Give sealed copies to a few trusted people to be opened just in case. There are other reasons besides death for needing help with one's affairs. Mental illness is one.

10. Emergency procedures can be prepared for fires, floods, power outages, epidemics, invasions, unemployment, etc. Listing what should be done helps call attention to what preparations and supplies should be provided. Thinking ahead with a deliberate, cool head beats frantic scrambling in a state of emotional shock.

## A PRACTICAL PHILOSOPHY NEEDED

What we think about what is happening may be of critical importance. Some attitudes give comfort and meaning, some cause unnecessary suffering. Perhaps someday our society will standardize on some optimum, mature, realistic attitudes. Meanwhile families, churches and study groups can sift through popular ideas and select some which seem meaningful to them.

## DEATH

1. *Miscellaneous.* Christian traditions, such as that the body must be buried in anticipation of the Resurrection and Judgment; cremation is out; one's spirit may go directly to the "house of many mansions"; it is God's will; and so on.

2. *Spiritualism.* "After this change called death" we find ourselves in the spirit world where individual conditions are somewhat similar to the life situation just left. Consciousness and personality continue without the body.

3. *Karma.* This theory includes reincarnation and explains that each spirit personality has eternal life-existence and finds itself in body after body. Advanced "mature" spirits are able to recall past lives and select conditions for their next one.

4. *One lifetime, period.* No previous lives; no survival of consciousness or personality after death; no spirit entity; no Judgment Day; no reward or punishment in the hereafter.

5. *"We buried Daddy today."* Visualizing the earthly remains of a loved one six feet under, cold, dark, lonely, where "the worms crawl in and the worms crawl out," is certainly a saddening pastime. Embalming and placement in a hermetically sealed time capsule do little to improve the picture. Something can be said for hastening the disintegration of the physical remains and disposing of them in a less specific manner, such as scattering the ashes after cremation. Is it really critical whether a body returns to dust in five hours or five thousand years?

## DISASTROUS LOSS

1. "I've lost everything! What's the use? Nothing matters!" We've heard of millionaires who committed suicide because they lost all their money. Others tell themselves philosophically, "I started from scratch before; I can do it again." Now, of course they have a head start with know-how and credit rating that they didn't have in the beginning.

2. Look what——did to me! I'm ruined, and it's all his fault!" Either "This proves that I'm a loser and can never make it" or "I'll get even with him if it's the last thing I do." This is one of the cornerstones of our legal system, isn't it? "It's okay to punish someone for his wrongdoing." But is it emotionally healthy to hold a grudge for months or years watching for a chance at revenge? Bitterness is a low-scale trap.

3. Psycho-cybernetics is powerful medicine. People in grief are in emotional shock, thus very susceptible to suggestion. Mental-image pictures can become very real. Thus phrases that we repeat to ourselves and conditions that we imagine or visualize do much to determine present and future emotions. A negative philosophy can bring on years of unnecessary emotional suffering. (See chap. 12 on Psycho-cybernetics.)

## LONELINESS

Many people have never known true love, since none of the people they have known were affectionate or lovable. But everyone has known loneliness. Color it cold and wet and dark. It is being outside, always the victim, always the loser, always the have-not. Warm emotions starve and ache and ferment in our guts when there is nobody out there who cares.

People need "terminals" just as electric circuits do. A "people terminal" both receives and sends a sort of love energy. If it isn't hooked up, nothing goes in and nothing goes out. A person without a terminal goes on breathing, but he often wonders why. Life doesn't seem very valuable without a buddy. *Everybody needs somebody.*

Intimacy is an infringement on personal privacy. It will cost you some freedom. But whatever the cost, it's worth it!

## IDEAS FOR PREVENTION

—Teach the slogan "Everybody needs somebody."

—Sponsor a community lonely-hearts club. Lots of lonely folks don't know how or where to meet new friends.

—Sponsor charm schools for girls and boys. Sponsor dancing classes, community choirs and bands and other nice places for people to meet.

—Point out to lonely people, "To be valued, one has to be valuable," that is, courteous, cooperative, interesting and interested.

—Sponsor more service/social clubs for military camps, prisons, hospitals, trade schools, single parents, and so on.

—Revive old-fashioned matchmaking. Friends should help friends find "somebody."

—Don't let yourself admit, "Nobody cares about me." If you suspect it is true, get busy! Almost anybody is better than nobody!

CHAPTER 19

# *Successful Learning*

Assume for the moment that when everyone achieves emotional maturity, there will no longer be *chronic* emotional suffering. Each person will strive to become his optimum self. Each person will gladly share community responsibilities. Everyone will be high on the gradient scale, with good health, good games, good problem-solving techniques and good citizenship.

These are the goals of our schools and churches. They strive to educate young people so that they will be able to earn a good living, lead meaningful lives and live together in brotherhood. But something is wrong! Few people are happy in their vocations. Few homes are serene and intimate. Private, public and professional morality codes are nebulous.

Are these goals and the formulas for reaching them valid?

Is it even possible for every adult to achieve emotional maturity?

Does emotional maturity (being high-scale) really guarantee good health, a satisfying career, an affectionate home, and so on?

Is education **the answer?**

Theoretically all answers are Yes. Isn't it obvious, however, that education as we know it today isn't successful? No matter how many mathematical formulas, historical dates and quotations from Shakespeare are memorized, students grow up confused about morality and patriotism, uncertain about choosing a career, disenchanted with their environment and groping for a self-image. Many hate school, read and write poorly, resist authority, have a short attention span, find almost everything boring except danger and violence. It almost seems that schools are teaching emotional immaturity and that a few children grow up right in spite of the system.

People who are unable or unwilling to learn are clumsy,

frustrated, unproductive and inadequate. In modern communities people who can't or won't learn are liabilities, extra useless bodies to be fed, clothed, sheltered and entertained.

Satisfying careers require the acquisition of abundant data and techniques, far more in the space age than was required or even dreamed of in the horse-and-buggy days. Understanding and technical skills are no longer optional luxuries.

Learning means to:

—Acquire knowledge, skill, understanding, perspective.

—Obtain wisdom, practical know-how, ability, a useful trade.

—Investigate, research, practice, memorize.

—Comprehend the nature of, appreciate importance and significance, realize fully the inner working principles.

—Develop intuition and cognition, intellectual vision, the power of apprehending relationships and making inferences from them.

—Acquire sufficient specialized information and skills to be useful.

"Useful" means:

—Satisfactory, favorable, prosperous accomplishment.

—Achieving a desired goal; finishing what needed to be done.

## EMOTIONAL PROBLEMS CAUSED BY INSUFFICIENT LEARNING

—Illiteracy, school dropouts, unemployable persons.

—Reluctant students and employees: unhappy and unwilling.

—Frustration caused by impotence; inability to solve problems.

—Accidents from ignorance: pregnancy, crime, drugs, disease.

—Low achievement caused by a lack of good coaching.

—Loneliness from a lack of social skills.

—Lack of leadership, wise planning and responsibility.

—Poverty.

—Self-pity, chronic low morale, inferiority complex.

—Family troubles, delinquency.

It seems true that "everyone does the best he knows how"

and that "most people are willing to do what they know how to do." People are clumsy because they don't know how to be skillful. Many high schools and colleges seem to overemphasize the importance of memorizing names, dates, theories in science, formulas in math, famous quotations and foreign languages. Students may graduate without being able to balance a checkbook, prepare food or start a balky engine.

A student may be a whiz at memorizing data from books and lectures, thereby earning fine grades, yet the course material may be irrelevant and useless in everyday life; he may forget it soon after the course is passed.

Successful learning may be quite different from memorizing enough stuff to pass tests. Memorizing data and vocabularies is important, of course, and that is what pays off *in school*. But here is what must be learned to be successful in the adult world:

—Obtain a diploma, degree, certificate or license in preparation for employment.

—Become engrossed, absorbed, in some art or craft which may be useful, profitable and satisfying.

—Enjoy learning. A successfully educated man goes on studying and learning for the rest of his life. He enjoys exploring new ideas and subjects. He is confident that he can look up or figure out just about anything. He dares to take on unusual jobs, certain that he knows how to learn whatever will be required.

—Communicate. He needs to know how to read easily; write intelligently, sketch and type; speak in public, use a microphone for radio or P.A. system; drive a car, make minor repairs; find an address in a strange city; use the telephone for DDD; use the various postal services; etc.

There is a long list of things everybody needs to know that aren't usually taught in school. . . .

A moron can't learn. He is a pitiful sight, unable to care for himself. A person who can learn but will not is no less to be pitied.

Is willingness an essential factor in learning? Not necessarily. Learning can result via fear, pain, hypnosis, suggestion, observation, mimicry and experiencing accidental events. High levels of

| | Students | Learning | Teaching |
|---|---|---|---|
| 12 | GENIUS: insatiable thirst to explore great ideas. | KNOWS: keen intuition, excellent common sense, cognites on solution soon after posing a question. | WISE COUNSELOR: provides space and direction for self-teaching. Suggests challenging adventures. |
| 11<br>10 | GOOD STUDENT: enjoys learning, wholehearted participation with the system, eager. | DOING AND LOOKING: does deliberate research; performs experiments. Learns easily. | COACH: supervises suitable learning projects, poses timely questions. Resourceful guide. |
| 9<br>8 | AVERAGE STUDENT: gets some pleasure from some subjects; submits to the system; most interest in extra-curricular. | LOOKING: observes spontaneous events and phenomena. Has cycles of easy learning and desire to participate. | AVERAGE TEACHER: follows lesson plan; offers emotional First Aid and personal counseling; alert waiting for interest. |
| 7<br>6 | HOSTILE STUDENT: reluctant compliance, resists the system; arrogance may mask a keen mind. | DOING: learns best by practice drills and mimicry. | TASKMASTER: authoritative, aggressive, terse, demands performance, keen awareness of all deficiencies. |
| 5<br>4 | FEARFUL, SHY, MARGINAL: nervous, tries hard. | MEMORIZES: observes in class, watches TV, reads OK, short attention span. | SHOUTS, THREATENS, OVERWHELMS: utilizes physical punishment; gives long assignments; may garble classroom lectures. |
| 3<br>2 | CLUMSY, INADEQUATE: seldom tries. | ATTENTION IS DISPERSED: can learn simple things by mimicry, suggestion and pain. | MOCK TEACHING: no teaching, no classroom discipline, no homework, no tests, just a kind of custodian system for bodies. |
| 1 | HOPELESSLY UNABLE: | STUPID: doesn't know what's going on. Doesn't care. | |

advanced arts or technical skills most certainly require some willingness to endure the many months of memorizing and practicing.

Learning is a preparation for good games. When good games are apparent, either as part of learning or surely promised for the future, learning is a satisfying, self-rewarding adventure.

Learning fits a person for a satisfying adulthood. He knows who he is. He senses continuous personal growth. He finds ways to fulfill himself.

Proper learning promotes good ARC (love). Good ARC makes learning easy. A student seems to tune in to a parent or teacher with whom he has high Affinity. If the subject matter is relevant and presented in easy logical steps, the Reality will be agreeable. Communication must be efficient and reliable: the ability to read and write is vital, as are good vision and hearing. Where Reality and Communications are good, Affinity will always be found. We all have fond memories of those teachers who worked us the hardest, who insisted that we apply attention to learn and understand.

The ideal teaching role of parent or teacher is to create situations where learning is easily possible and to maintain the games condition. The optimum student must reach for learning. The teacher places learning within his reach. Some students will not reach, of course, since they are low-scale. Memorizing and enforced rules must be used with them until they mature up-scale.

Successful learning is a source of pride, profit and fascinating adventure. Public schools are often unsuccessful. Thousands of students develop serious emotional symptoms while in high school and college. Millions of people refuse to avail themselves of night school and correspondence courses because of previous bitter experiences in schools.

## WHAT IS WRONG WITH EDUCATION?

1. Wrong gradient. Students are not all alike! Placing a slow student in a fast class or a fast student in a slow class will handicap him.

## Successful Learning

2. Wrong age group. Studies by the Gesell Institute revealed that there is a 50-50 chance that your child is at least one grade ahead of the one he should be in to do his best. See "Your Child May Be in the Wrong Grade at School," *Reader's Digest,* Aug., 1966. Also see the book *School Readiness* by Drs. Ilg and Ames.

3. Teacher problems. Some teachers just have poor classroom techniques; some have personality problems of their own. It is pretty hard to enjoy a class with a teacher who hates teaching but needs the money.

4. Distractions. Lack of class discipline, too much horseplay, classrooms too crowded, no atmosphere for learning. Many classes would be improved 100 percent if the 10 percent of the bodies who came to play were sent somewhere else to do it.

5. Poverty. Malnutrition, poor clothes, cold schools, etc. It is too much to ask for kids to be interested in books when the present-time problems are about to overwhelm them.

6. Lack of motivation. No goal, no games, no suitable rewards.

7. Irrelevant subject material. Mental sawdust, wasted effort.

8. Compulsive, overwhelming, autocratic, impersonal authority; unwilling attendance.

9. Saturation. (1) Too many classes, too much homework, too much school, too much sports, too much part-time work, cause physical tiredness "in the bones." (2) One-way flow: Continuous lectures, with no recitations or discussions; all study (inflow) with no tests (outflow) eventually blocks further input, shutting off attention and interest. The human mind works best with inflow and outflow cycles.

10. Missed datum. If a student misses an important point, a theory, formula or key word, his subconscious gets hung up—stuck. Part of his attention must remain puzzling over that little mystery forever, or until it is explained and understood. If a student continues to miss basic ideas, each of which traps some of his attention units, he will soon find that he is unable to study easily. The pleasure of it is gone.

11. Emotional shock. Many, many events in and out of school may cause some degree of emotional shock to a student,

thus putting him out of touch with reality to some degree. Family trouble at home is a well-known cause. Changing teachers or schools abruptly may affect some students traumatically. Good students who seem to suddenly turn off are in shock. Review chapter 9.

12. Pushing students into advanced classes far beyond their latent ability. Many students have no taste for, and are not suited for, academic scholastic studies and college-level work. Their need may be for apprenticeship in manual or technical skills.

13. Lack of good study habits or of a good place to study; lack of self-discipline.

14. Poor communication skills. Poor reading, poor writing, excessive shyness in public speaking and reciting, unwillingness to ask for help, being overwhelmed with fear during a test, clumsy social habits, rudeness, arrogance.

15. Trained to rebel. Thousands of children are trained at home to resist any authority and oppose the Establishment. They have a thing about obeying direct orders; they seem to be compelled to procrastinate or refuse. They hate morality, custom and self-control. Sneering at the prospects of becoming well-informed and skillful, they prefer sensuous activities—rough sports, speed and danger. These people are vague about value judgments and usually make decisions based on emotional whims. They are unwilling to make long-term commitments; they have a short attention span. Usually this "emotional set" is learned at home. This is the flavor of their home and neighborhood culture. These are the "devil kids" who would rather do almost anything besides play school.

## ESSAY

Dear Mr. Editor:

Since school budgets are a perpetual problem across our nation, I propose some changes in our educational philosophy.

Let us consider our school tax money as a fund to be invested to yield the highest returns possible. What returns can we expect?

—A perpetual crop of young adults to serve our society as doctors, teachers, engineers, social leaders, businessmen, etc. (professional people).

—A middle class which is able and willing to sustain a high standard of economic and social responsibility.

—A "utility" class, able and willing to be good sweepers, laborers, privates, etc. There's nothing wrong with being a good laborer. The point is that some people have no desire or talent for years of technical apprenticeship or academic studies.

Experts tell us that we are behind in our crops of professionals. Other reports indicate that a certain percentage of children in high school either can't or won't learn but just sit in class hating every minute of it. They are wasting their time and our investment in them. Worse, they create little dark clouds of emotional static which jam the learning the real students are trying to soak up.

We all agree that every American child should have the right and opportunity to get as much education as he wants. Perhaps we can go so far as to say that each child has a moral duty to get as much education as he can possibly use. But does it serve any good purpose to force young people to be tortured in classrooms against their will, overwhelming them with subjects for which they have no need, while they dilute the teaching facilities which are really needed by the bona fide students?

Let's take a giant step towards solving our teacher and classroom shortage by dropping the 10 per cent of the young people who are not in school to learn. If they must have professional baby sitters until they are eighteen, let's set up apprenticeship programs for them, such as the C.C.C. and N.Y.A. camps, to put them to work at various trades doing something useful and learning self-respect.

It is neither logical nor fair to adulterate the student body of a high school with uncooperative, unscholarly, untalented children who are unable or unwilling to benefit from the expensive facilities provided for them. It degrades a high-school diploma to force it on a person who doesn't want it and hasn't earned it. Schools should be for students. Let's provide other more suitable activities for the other youngsters.

## OTHER IDEAS FOR DISCUSSION

*Education isn't successful if:*
—The student isn't happy and optimistic.
—He lacks moral convictions and a sense of common decency.
—He isn't qualified and confident in a trade or profession.
—He lacks technical knowledge needed to set up and manage a home and family.
—He is weak in some important facet of emotional maturity.
—He is indifferent or derisive about law, civic duties, national patriotism.
—He is generally discourteous and arrogant.
—He frequently jeopardizes his and others' personal health and physical safety.
—He denounces *all* religious or philosophical creeds.
—He ignores the rights and needs of future generations.

*Is this preparation for adult living?* He passed his intermediate algebra and Latin, obtaining knowledge and skills he may never use. He did *not* learn typing, public speaking, mechanical drawing, basic law, basic economics, how to care for a car or how to use an electronic multimeter for testing lamps, fuses, batteries and motors.

She passed geometry and physics. She does *not* know how to start a balky auto engine, balance a checkbook, pack a faucet, can food or deliver a baby.

*Successful learning is fun.* If you learn right, you will enjoy reading and taking courses all of your life. Years spent in school will be only the beginning of a lifetime of exploration, adventure and challenge. Prior to 1920 some of America's greatest leaders were self-educated, many going no further than the eighth grade.

It is an ironic dilemma that about half of the America public is facing two choices: (1) submit to the public educational system, practice self-control and endure authoritative discipline or (2) quit school, submit to the public-welfare system, practice self-pity and endure the boredom and oppressive indignity of occasional menial employment. Why are so many millions of people unhappy when forced to do (learn) what the other millions do for the fun of it?

We can't learn a modern technology without studying the theories and vocabulary. Book learning—theories and vocabulary—are only about 50 per cent of a science or technology. The other half must come from doing and using. Therefore study does not necessarily result in ability, familiarity or skill in performance. Apprenticeship combined with book theory should be an ideal way to balance doing with learning, to continuously relate the study material with the practical application.

Many teachers ignore the relative importance of the data being presented. Studying foolish or unrelated material dulls the ability to study. This was formerly defended in the name of "mental exercise." There are other mental exercises which are much more fun and creative.

Frequent little rewards are useful in training animals—and people. Small wins and easy quizzes help the student sense that he is progressing in the right direction.

When a willing student can't study, the trouble may be:
—the gradient is too steep or not steep enough.
—he missed some fundamentals.
—he had an ARC break with the teacher or with the text.
—he has an unrelated emotional problem; he's in emotional shock.

What he seems to be having trouble with is not the real trouble. He is beyond the trouble point by the time he realizes something is wrong. In counseling you have to go back to a point where the student was not having trouble, then come forward in time to find where the trouble started. He will probably not know when it started, and counseling skill is needed to find the exact cause, word or idea.

A missed datum or an ARC break may result in physical reactions such as a pale blank expression or a faint hysteria. Too steep a gradient causes confusion and an inability to act.

*Education should lead to practical skills.* When it comes to survival, or even playing life games, what you can actually do is more important than how much miscellaneous information you can remember.

Too many courses are superficial—intending to introduce the student to a subject, but not leading to a working knowledge. Later, if he can't use it, he'll forget it. So why teach it? At these prices schools should be teaching material the students either want or need, not stuff that is unwanted and bound to be forgotten.

*Find the student.* A real student is more than a body sitting at a desk. A student (*a*) wants to learn, (*b*) is able to learn and (*c*) is learning. Not all young bodies sitting at schoolroom desks are students. Many don't really give a damn about learning. A few are not able to learn. And finally, all too often the teacher isn't teaching. How many professors read their notes or give their lectures in a mechanical fashion, not knowing or caring whether any of those young bodies are actually tuned in? He's doing his thing; it's entirely up to them to do theirs!

Find the student where he's at. If you really care about communicating, you have to transmit on his frequency. You have to speak his language; lead his thinking from *his* known to the unknown. Generally it is up to the teacher, who is older and wiser, to establish rapport—good ARC—with the student.

*Vocabulary.* Words are thinking tools. They are a sort of shorthand, symbols for real things, ideas, theories, concepts, phenomena and significances.

*Psycho-cybernetics.* A student should have a clear personal purpose. He should be able to visualize a goal that seems to be important enough to invest time and effort in. Teachers love eager students.

"Memorize this, memorize that; pass the test, pass the course; get the credits, get the diploma. Forget half of it if you want to. Never mind that you aren't going to college anyhow. Never mind that there are a thousand things about daily living you will have to find out the hard way. . . ."

Let's try being student-oriented.

CHAPTER 20

# *Work*

Work can be:
—Drudgery, exertion, labor, task, compulsive duty; monotonous, boring, tiring occupation; hard, distasteful.
—Doing what is needed, accomplishing useful results, creating wealth or beauty.

## EMOTIONAL PROBLEMS INVOLVING WORK

In North America at least half the population never knew anyone who *liked* work. To them work is a necessary evil, though somewhat less evil than extreme poverty and hunger. On the other hand, there are people who enjoy their chosen career most of the time, and a very few people who are so engrossed in their work that they indulge themselves in it day and night, weekends and holidays. Their occupation seems to be a series of delightful tasks, fascinating problems to be solved, games of life. We are told that famous musicians, circus performers, research scientists and inventors dedicate their lives to some art or cause which seems vitally worthwhile to them. Many schoolteachers, nurses, doctors and ministers find their careers immensely satisfying. Probably most of the Peace Corps volunteers join up for the fun of it. Not all work is bad; some people like work. Everybody likes the good things that work makes possible: food, clothing, shelter, toys.

*Work is not hard, but thinking makes it so!* Consider the tremendous energy expended and the hundreds or thousands of hours of preparation and practice required to become a champion swimmer or tennis player or musician. Hard work and boring repetition are not the true culprits. People are *taught* that all work is hard, painful and oppressive. They never knew anyone who enjoyed his career and worked for the fun of it. Of course some work is tiring and frustrating. Many, many people *are* overworked and underpaid; there *are* arrogant bosses, bigoted union leaders and cruel plant managers. Work *is* hard under low-scale conditions.

## MANY BOSSES WERE TRAINED TO BE OPPRESSIVE!

They were trained to shout and growl. They think that's what bosses are supposed to do. If you are going to be a drill sergeant, you must learn to shout commands like a drill sergeant. In some industries, if you don't shout and growl, your workers won't think you mean it. Soft words might not be heard at all.

There are many quaint sayings which have become accepted as standard operating procedures: "If you give a man an inch, he'll want a foot," "Do *something,* even if it's wrong," "There are three ways to do things: the right way, the wrong way and our way." Some bosses insist on mediocrity, rejecting all suggestions from long habit. One popular cop-out that management still uses is, "If you don't like the way we do things here, you know what you can do."

## THOUSANDS ARE POORLY TRAINED FOR THEIR JOBS

Getting along by luck or bluff causes fear and anxiety. Many quite able and well-educated people are properly hired for well-paying jobs and then turned loose. "Pick it up as you go along," "Play it by ear," "There's really not much to it,"—these are cop-outs for not furnishing job descriptions, tech manuals and good on-the-job training. The able people do somehow manage to get the job done, at the cost of high emotional strain and weeks or months of fumbling, false starts, booboos and unnecessary crises. Many good employees quit because of poor coaching and on-the-job training. Remember the ARC rule? When communication is inadequate, affinity and reality will be low. By contrast a stern taskmaster communicates with such certainty that reality is high. There is never any doubt about what the boss wants! He may not be warm and friendly, but his workers do respect him and trust him and turn to him for help and advice, even about personal affairs.

## THOUSANDS OF JOBS ARE SEASONAL OR TEMPORARY

Migrant farm workers, for instance, and military families have special emotional problems. Field engineers, traveling salesmen and newsmen live out of a suitcase. All of these people must make more critical decisions every day. Their environment is usually changing, unfamiliar and to some degree hostile. A barracks or hotel room can never be as comforting and secure as one's own kitchen and living room. Recreation in a strange town must be more high-powered and superficial than puttering in one's own garden or playing cards with old friends. Frequent changes of homes and schools are especially traumatic for wives and children.

## HALF THE LABOR FORCE IS LOW-SCALE

Here is the gradient scale of workers (See chap. 3). Remember, the scale is set up so that "average" is halfway up. Half the workers are below the mid-scale median. There is lots of room for improvement.

High-scale people enjoy working; can be trusted to use good common sense; learn easily; don't get too shaken if they have to change; come up with good suggestions for doing things easier and better; usually avoid problems or solve unavoidable problems themselves.

Low-scale people are just the opposite. They shun work, sometimes act stupid, resist the idea of studying or any kind of self-improvement. They actually find ways to pay money to hurt themselves! They are allergic to change; their "suggestions" are mostly gripes. If the unexpected can happen, they'll help it to happen. They are angry, fearful, unskilled by nature, in spite of ideal working conditions. They find ways to foul up even a good job.

A high-scale worker can be worth ten times as much as a

# PERSONAL

This chart will help you visualize your personal goals. Just for the fun of it, read down each column and pick out your square. Place a mark where you would rate yourself. When you finish, connect each mark with a solid line to form a sort of graph.

|  | Job Knowledge | Quality of Work | Cooperation | Initiative | Work Output | Reliability |
|---|---|---|---|---|---|---|
| 12 | Expert in his job | Neat Accurate Complete Efficient | Always helpful Volunteers | Many useful suggestions Self-starter | Always above requirements | Certain dependability |
| 11 | Good knowledge of related jobs | | | | | |
| 10 | | | | | | Fully responsible |
| 9 | Well informed | Usually good Corrects errors | Meets others halfway | Handles own job easily | Consistently good | Usually reliable Sincere effort |
| 8 | | | | | | |
| 7 | | | | | | |
| 6 | Satisfactory | Improvement needed | Touchy Opinionated Narrow-minded | Needs supervision often | Sometimes good, but not too reliable | Close supervision needed |
| 5 | Limited knowledge | | | | | |
| 4 | | | | | | |
| 3 | Doesn't know job | Many errors Careless Incomplete Liability | Antagonistic Constant friction Tblmaker. | Must be told what to do Mischievous | Always below job requirements Spoiler | Careless, easily distracted and confused |
| 2 | | | | | | |
| 1 | Unwilling to learn | | | | | |

## ABILITY

The goal of our training program is to help you move that graph up. High-toned people usually enjoy their responsibilities, and they find ways to make life more pleasant for everyone. Learning to be high-toned is learning to be more alive. Since you have joined our "team" why not "play" to win!

### DO YOUR PART—DO YOUR BEST.

| Judgment | Personal Appearance | Communications | Leadership | Potential Success | Emotion |
|---|---|---|---|---|---|
| Decisions based on intelligent analysis | Always well groomed, personable | Persuasive, fluent, confident, clarifies, simplifies | Inspiring Effective leader | Excellent<br><br>Very good | Eager<br><br>Strong interest |
| Uses good common sense | Usually neat | Writes and speaks well | Satisfactory<br><br>Seeking improvement | Good<br><br>Fair | Some interest<br><br>Content |
| Judgment OK on routine matters | Sometimes neglects personal appearance | Shy, self-conscious Avoids speaking | Occasionally effective | Poor<br><br>Often fails | Bored Indifferent<br><br>Open resentment |
| Erratic judgment Jumps at conclusions | Slovenly; no concern for appearances | Inarticulate<br><br>Illiterate | Ineffective as a leader | Usually fails<br><br>Total liability | Anger<br><br>Inner hostility Fear |

low-scale "body." In some cases the high-scale skilled technician is able to accomplish work which is absolutely impossible for the lazy, arrogant, illiterate helper. Even if they were picking apples or painting barns, the high-scale man would get more done easier and get into less trouble than the helper.

What is wrong with good honest hard work? Nothing is wrong with work. Low-toned people can resist, denounce and foul up *anything*. There may be a hundred ways to defame a vocation, and they will find them. Logic would indicate that most of the problems of work can be avoided or eliminated by providing effective emotional therapy for all people who are not happily employed.

## PROFESSIONAL EMOTIONAL THERAPY IS NEEDED FOR THE HARD-CORE UNEMPLOYED

Studies have shown that most high-school dropouts are smart enough to learn; they seem to be turned off. There are other psychological problems which may blight a man for successful employment. Few people can correct such problems for themselves, even if they recognize and acknowledge them. Skillful therapy is needed. Even though relatively expensive in time and money, successful therapy is a profitable investment considering the sum a steady worker earns in a lifetime. To deny people the therapy they need can result in high costs of delinquency, crime, welfare and emotional illness.

Visualize a young person with one or more of the following emotional handicaps:

| | | |
|---|---|---|
| Chronic tiredness | Chain of failures | No confidence |
| Chronic grief | Guilt | Thirst for revenge |
| Arrogance | Hate | Wrong perspective |
| No sense of time | Poor self-image | Misinformation |
| Poor memory | Poor social habits | Nervousness |
| Phobias, allergies | Mean streak | Clumsiness |
| Perpetual anger | Covert hostility | Bad body odor |
| Blemished skin | Physical handicap | Quick temper |
| No personal goal | Speech impediment | Allergy to authority |

# Work

The list seems formidable. Therapy may be difficult but is not impossible. *Something can be done.*

## SUB-GOALS OF PSYCHOTHERAPY

Maximum motivation:
—Introduce "psychic income."
—Establish meaningful personal goals.
—Develop a productive self-image.
Overcome hostility:
—Self-pity from being a have-not.
—Resistance to discipline and authority.
—Poverty indoctrination from peers (think "poor").
Detect and overcome traumatic childhood experiences:
—Harsh discipline or none.
—Antisocial or non-cooperative habits.
—Unhappy school and work experience.
—Rough social life; no satisfying hobbies.
—Negative thinking patterns about self, grownups, government.
Detect and overcome early employment misfortunes:
—Job hunting and interviewing traumas.
—Confusion, uncertainty and fear from poor OJT and indoctrination on new jobs.
—Hope for independence fails when lack of thrift and poor judgment result in excessive debts even while employed.
Reverse anti-social, non-productive sub-culture orientation.
Establish a personal plan for emergency Emotional First Aid.

## PSYCHO-CYBERNETICS AT WORK

Purposeful positive thinking habits are vitally important to achieving a satisfying vocational career. Think of the power that could be turned on by repeating this chant every morning:

This is the place I want to be. This is what I want to do. Working here is usually quite satisfying. I am using my skills to do what needs to be done, and to solve problems. They need me. I am learning and growing in my career; I am getting recognition and advancement. They know I am earning my pay. It is a dignified job, and I am proud to tell people I work here. My job is a challenge; I must keep on my toes and do my best because my team is depending on me to do my part.

## HIGH MORALE

High morale indicates a good worker on a good job. It is a prevailing mood and spirit conducive to willing and dependable performance; steady self-control; courageous, determined conduct despite danger and privations; a conviction of being in the right and on the way to success; faith in the cause or program and in the leadership. It is a confident, aggressive, resolute, often buoyant spirit of wholehearted cooperation in common effort, often attended by zeal, self-sacrifice. It is indomitable, unconquerable, invincible.

(See also "Personal Standard of Excellence," p. 69.)

## CAN YOU DO THE WORK OF TWENTY MEN?

Probably not. It is entirely possible that you could help twenty men accomplish twice as much, that is, become twice as efficient. Actually, merely doubling a person's efficiency is a rather modest goal under certain circumstances. A tenfold improvement is sometimes a practical goal. Such an improvement can easily change drudgery into a meaningful satisfying vocation; it can make the difference between a losing proposition and a fine profit.

There are at least three ways to do this kind of magic. (1) You could give a man (twenty men) better tools. Instead of a hand hoe, give him a wheel hoe; instead of a paintbrush, give him a roller or a paint sprayer; instead of buckets to haul water, give him a pump and some pipes. (2) Teach him valuable technology. A farmer can easily improve the yield of a field five times using modern seeds, fertilizer and irrigation, which is much easier than plowing and cultivating five fields, and the finer crop may bring a premium price too. Every occupation and industry has its labor-saving schemes and short cuts, and over half of the workers don't know them! When it comes to starting balky engines, fixing dead radios and preventing a disease epidemic, a modest contribution of appropriate know-how can do more than twenty or a hundred unskilled willing hands. Teaching people how to read and providing appropriate books are practical ways a few people can make an astonishing impact on the productive efficiency of a large group.

(3) The third kind of magic is morale therapy. Visualize a gradient scale of morale versus worker efficiency. At the top of the scale is 100 per cent, of course: the worker uses the best tools and methods, his work has zero defects, his teamwork is fine, he anticipates problems and solves them easily. At the bottom of the scale is 0 per cent efficiency: the worker does little work, which usually has to be undone and corrected; he disturbs his fellow workers; he is accident-prone. Theoretically half the workers are less than 50 per cent efficient because of their emotional immaturity, bad attitudes and non-cooperative habits. They would rather "fight than switch" to improved methods, better teamwork and keeping their minds on their jobs.

What do you think? How much more work can an eager beaver do than a disgruntled warm body? Make a list of ten ways a boss can invalidate and beat down an eager beaver, until he loses his spirit and refuses to take any further personal interest in the work. What could a new boss do to make a group of warm bodies into a sharp team?

## ZERO DEFECTS PROGRAM

The Navy thinks it pays to do jobs right the first time. Some, like building a submarine, can't be tested and repaired. Either the sub is built right or it stays sunk! Perfect work requires high morale: men must *care enough* to do their best and to live up to very high personal standards. High efficiency doesn't cost—it pays!

## THE HUMAN FACTOR IN INDUSTRY

Discussing the need for perfection in many multimillion-dollar industries, such as large airports, submarines, and our vast

Early Warning Defense Systems, a chief engineer pointed out that people are the weakest link!

When designing a billion-dollar industry, engineers can specify the most reliable materials, they can design near-perfect machines, they can provide automatic spare systems for instant backup. They can now engineer near-perfect plants which will operate about 98 per cent of the time.

That isn't good enough! A 2 per cent failure rate is outrageous in the telephone, electric-power and food-preserving industries. Two per cent is 7.3 days per year—175 hours. Our D.E.W. line would be almost useless for giving us fifteen minutes' early warning of an enemy attack if it operated only 98 per cent of the time.

The last 2 per cent, the critical ingredient that makes the difference between 98 per cent and perfection is the human factor. The installers, the operators and the maintenance technicians must care enough to do their part, and do their best *all of the time.*

Such dedication and esprit de corps is supernormal. Look again at the gradient scale of ability. Normal isn't "very good" or "excellent"; it is just getting by. Ships go down and planes crash almost weekly because someone didn't care enough about some routine detail.

Someday Emotional First Aiders in industry will (1) prevent unnecessary emotional situations and (2) devise Standard Operating Procedures for monitoring traumatic personal situations and dangerous employee attitudes; and (3) industry will reverse its hands-off tradition and proclaim its right and duty to provide emotional therapy.

## ADDITIONAL IDEAS

*Noise* is an important factor in work. It can influence concentration, tiredness, morale and even physical health.

*Leadership training* could be improved by establishing some sort of confidential feedback from the workers to the big boss. It is common practice for foremen to fill out personnel efficiency reports on their men; it's sort of a report-card system. Many foremen are clumsy leaders and create unnecessary emotional problems daily, but there is no way to record or correct their inefficiencies. Sometimes some of the workers have had more book training in leadership than their boss, who may have worked his way up the ladder without formal leadership training. In other words, some workers are qualified to make constructive criticisms; and there should be a procedure to get their good ideas into the front office.

*Luxury* stimulates ambition and motivation. Sometimes it pays to dangle a carrot before a lazy mule.

*Psychic income* is a little-known treasure. Some jobs seem to be worth while, meaningful and vital in spite of low dollar wages. Psychic fringe benefits include realizing a worthy challenge; being wanted and appreciated; sensing progress in one's vocation —getting raises and promotions, for instance; having good games and high morale; seeing a job through to a profitable and satisfying finish. Many highly paid people quit good jobs because the psychic income is too low. Money isn't everything, and some of the best things in life *are* free.

If it became possible to change your career, and you could become anything you wished, what would you really like to be?

## IS UNEMPLOYMENT AN IMAGINARY BOGEY?

There may be a hundred ways for government, industry and labor to foul up commerce and cause a real depression. There is, however, another more constructive view of the facts.

Wealth can be produced by combining the following ingredients: raw materials, manpower and skill, leadership and good ideas. America has an abundance of raw materials. It has manpower it doesn't know what to do with. Technical skills are plentiful. Good leadership is in short supply, but the shortage could be remedied; the critical shortage is in the good-idea department.

There is a long list of nice things this country would like to have: millions of new homes; finer, cheaper food; pollution control; erosion control; faster, safer transportation; better medical services; a reduction in crime; thousands of new mental-health clinics; and plenty of new recreation facilities. There is a periodic alarm about the critical shortage of gold and silver. Ha! Most of the gold and silver is still in the hills near the old mines where the old-timers found theirs. If our nation wants gold badly enough, we've got the manpower and technical skills to dig it out.

The 747 jet liner, 50 million color TV sets, sending a man to the moon . . . "impossible" only twenty years ago! Unemployment is a waste of potential wealth and luxury. Much depends on whether this nation can bring forth some great ideas and train some inspired leaders.

## CHAPTER 21

# *Tiredness*

"Tiredness" is being weary, exhausted, fatigued, without usual or necessary energy, without vitality, without vigor, having no ambition.

### THREE CLASSES OF TIREDNESS

—"Honest" tiredness from long or tedious work or play.
—Physical problems: malnutrition, excessive cold or heat; it is a common symptom accompanying all medical illness.
—Psychological problems: negative thinking, boredom, engrams, confusion, despair, hopelessness.

### EMOTIONAL PROBLEMS CAUSED BY CHRONIC TIREDNESS

—Poor spirit, no desire for humor, sport or games.
—Poor communication; grumpy, terse, stingy.
—Poor planning, procrastination; "don't care."
—Lack of responsibility for environment; it is shabby and cluttered.
—A tired person is non-competitive, under-achieving, helpless.

Honest tiredness is directly caused by overexertion, hard work and going without sleep. Staying up too late nights and getting up too early are sure ways to cause great emotional suffering during the day at work or school. Many people are addicted to night life and TV watching and overdraw their sleep accounts frequently. They are usually starved for sleep. Whatever they must do seems to be a burden. The cigarettes and coffee they consume for a lift eventually make matters worse. These people complain about the rat race, not knowing that they are causing it by being too tired to enjoy being alive.

Fun is giving or throwing energy away. No energy—no fun!

## SOME SOLUTIONS TO TIREDNESS

—Take intelligent care of your health; develop good living habits.

—Ration waking hours; sleep a little more—be a lot more alive while awake. If you borrow sleep for a big party, pay it back. Catch up by getting extra sleep the next night.

—Have a medical checkup to spot "iron-poor blood," weak thyroid, need for hormones, possibility of diabetes, etc. How is your blood sugar?

—Review your diet. Many people have poor eating habits. Some need vitamins and other food supplements. Some people should eat less at one time but eat more often to avoid drowsiness.

—Overweight? It is tiring to carry around thirty or forty superfluous pounds.

—Seek counseling to discover your emotional burden. What is it that is "like a millstone around your neck" or "hangs heavy over your head"?

—Study up on psycho-cybernetics. Positive thinking can do miracles.

—Change of pace. Maybe your problem is mostly boredom. There are many things in our daily schedule that can be changed easily: get a job transfer, adopt a new hobby, take a night-school course.

—Change of career. What would you really like to do? Could you possibly change careers so that your daily duties would seem more like playing at a hobby than working for a living?

—Take naps. Biographies show that many successful people have indulged themselves with naps in the afternoon or after supper, partly because of the pleasure of napping, and in order to store up extra energy for the next bout with adventure.

## VITALITY

A famous doctor recently began his lecture to two hundred students with a smile. His first remark was, "I'm worth a million dollars today." Everyone knew what he meant: buoyant health is

## Tiredness

more precious than a fortune. A healthy body is really worth having, worth working and studying for.

Continuing, he pointed out that a complete health program must have three phases: physical, mental and spiritual. Physical: fresh air, good food, sleep, exercise and cleanliness. Mental: knowledge about balanced diet, poisons, rules for First Aid, signs of trouble, supplementary foods and medicines, safety rules for work and play, prevention. Spiritual (and psychological): emotional maturity, positive thinking, a sense of security, a personal interest and goal in life, and a rational attitude toward a religious philosophy.

Compare a human being to an automobile:

—Physical: the parts must be properly shaped and fitted, and be made of the proper materials; fluids must be just right.

—Mental: the tune-up adjustments must be just right—spark timing, gas mixture, valve clearances, gears, voltages.

—Spiritual/psychological: an auto is useless or even dangerous unless controlled with skill and useful intention.

Isn't it obvious that abundant living is more than having a strong healthy body and a good education? The formula for vitality must include useful intention.

Get a clear picture of vitality in action:

—The athlete who knows the rules and has skill and energy to win.

—The boyfriend with ideas, ambition, thoughtfulness, courage and self-confidence.

—The girlfriend who knows a hundred ways to be a woman, who can make her man feel ten feet tall, who can make any house a home, any food a meal.

—The businessman who can find skill and materials to do a proud job.

—The leader whose followers always volunteer, who makes tough jobs seem to be fascinating games.

—The father who can seem to be a hero to his family.

—The teacher who makes learning seem like exciting adventure.

What do vitality and high morale have to do with "spiritual"?

I don't mean praying, hymn-singing, sin-confessing spiritual. I mean plenty-of-courage, be-a-good-citizen, fun-to-know, do-my-share, always-reliable-trustworthy, too-proud-to-accept-second-rate-performance-from-himself, glad-to-be-alive spiritual. Being filled with a really alive spirit.

Parents, you want the best for your children. You want them to have a healthy body without pain; a good education (lots of facts and diplomas); and vitality—the *will* to use what they have skillfully—to *care enough* to be useful. Some, with poor bodies and little education, have *cared enough,* have had enough spiritual vitality, to set brilliant examples of living. How can you inspire your children to become more alive?

We all know ways to become less alive: go without sleep, use drugs and alcohol, negative thinking, dull environment, and so on. Now make a list of factors which can bring new vitality, turn up the front burner and make life seem really worth living.

## CHAPTER 22

# *Family Counseling*

Family counseling is a rainbow of psychological services performed for a family group together, at the same time. At one end of the rainbow is premarital counseling, which is intended to be of a preventive nature. The other extreme is pre-divorce counseling, which is trying to prevent an emotional crisis from terminating in a family disaster. First Aiders are advised in ways to handle relatively small, spontaneous emotional problems in order to hasten self-therapy and prevent relatively simple issues from snowballing. Divorce talk is not a simple matter; it is a crisis and deserves the prompt attention of the best professional skill available: judge, minister, doctor, lawyer or social worker.

Professional counselors do very little Emotional First Aid; that is, people don't seek professional help until they really hurt and their situation seems unbearable and hopeless. There is much emotional suffering in families that never quite reaches the boiling point. Some of that suffering can be prevented, and some of it can be relieved or cured by training amateur counselors in Emotional First Aid. *Now* is so important, against waiting three weeks for an appointment.

Studies have shown that about 80 percent of all marriages are poor and that the individuals' needs are not being met. About 25 percent get divorced; 15 percent get legally separated; many spouses are adulterous; some just disappear—get lost; some fight frequently; and many more just smolder in covert hostility and loneliness. Some hurt inside so bad that they seek counseling. Many unhappy spouses survive together for the children's sake.

Whatever is wrong with families and marriages, psychiatrists and divorce courts are powerless to *prevent* the emotional problems. Prevention must come from a program which will teach everyone the principles of emotional maturity.

Consider a gradient scale of marriages: half the marriages would be below the median, in areas where anger, fear, guilt and hostility are the rule. Low-scale people are poorly informed and lack problem-solving techniques. High-scale people seem to have a monopoly on self-discipline, good ARC, logical reasoning powers and good problem-solving abilities.

Family counseling is an emergency service, intended to relieve the pressure in a family so that it won't blow apart. It is expected that the emergency will be over within six weekly sessions, hardly enough time to rebuild each member's personality. Continued optimum family conditions can be ensured only by raising all members up-scale toward emotional maturity, where they can all avoid emotional problems or work out their own solutions.

## WHAT A FAMILY COUNSELOR DOES

1. He writes down a systematic case history, listing the pros and cons of the family relationships. Each member gets to tell in his own words what he thinks is the main trouble, and he gets to hear the others tell it like it is. Where a family is filled with hostility, even this much communication may clear the air considerably.

2. If the symptom seems to be anger, the counselor can set up a bout, or debate, then referee the match, making use of the rules on anger (chap. 17).

3. ARC is always low in a problem family. (There wouldn't be a problem if ARC was high; see the article on ARC, p. 108.) The counselor coaches each member of the family on improved communication.

4. Often the counselor can see the real problem when the family can see only the symptoms. He may recommend that the family seek the professional aid of a lawyer, medical doctor, minister, psychiatrist or social agency.

5. Frequently a case history discloses that one or both spouses are clumsy at being spouse or parent because they don't know any better. They are doing what they saw their parents do, which was pitifully crude, mean, selfish, violent and immature. The

counselor uses techniques to help the parties see themselves and their actions, and coaches them in self-improvement.

6. The counselor certainly weaves the principles of Emotional First Aid into each session. He will probably give the older members of the family some homework to do between sessions. This may consist of reprints of magazine articles, case histories of people who had similar problems and perhaps questionnaires designed to help intelligent persons analyze their own situations.

7. The family is guided to look ahead, to foresee the outcome of the course they are on. Will it be reform school for an older child? Separation, divorce, poverty, disgrace, mental breakdown? Such bleak pictures are a powerful force in persuading people to make every effort to change their ways.

8. An important part of the program is to help the family decide on a plan for changing their daily lives. The plan will probably include a clear definition of home rules, a list of the duties of each member, and a statement of the goals they hope to achieve by the next session.

## THE PROBLEM CHILD

Virginia Satir, a leading family therapist and author, has set forth in her book *Conjoint Family Therapy* the concept that a troublesome child is not a neat little package of trouble but rather the dramatic symptom of a whole family in emotional pain.

Mrs. Satir has found that where husband and wife can be taught to respect and love each other, problems with the children seem to wither away, almost as if cut off from their source. Effective therapy results from listing the wayward child's symptoms, then aiming therapy efforts at the parents.

Dr. W. M. Brodey wrote: "When the parents are emotionally close, they can do no wrong in their 'management' of the patient. The child responds well to firmness, permissiveness, punishment, 'talking it out,' or any other management approach. When parents are emotionally divorced, any and all management approaches are equally unsuccessful.

"What can the fact that Father left home in a rage have to

do with little Johnny mussing his pants in school? It doesn't make sense." Johnny is suffering from a traumatic emotional shock. People in shock frequently do things to hurt themselves and those they love. They don't know why. They are very sorry. They lost control. They went a little bit crazy.

It appears that a child's psyche is tuned to the psyches of his parents. If their emotional life is turbulent, his will be too. He depends on them for survival and good communications. If their family unit is breaking up, so is his.

Do babies worry? Certainly five-year-olds do. We know that continuity of relationships is important. Rapid changing of stepparents, nurses or teachers makes it difficult for a young psyche to tune in and feel wanted. An inner aloneness may result. One child confided, "They don't care about me, just what to do with my body."

## HOW TO MAKE A CHILD "BAD"

All interpersonal communications have two parts: (1) Content. Verbal information, the actual literal meaning. (2) "Metamessage." The implied double meaning inferred by the tone of voice; a sort of sub-audible code for interpreting the double talk. (See "Metacom," p. 32.)

After long exposure to double-meaning slang and contradictory teasing and kidding, a child's ability to give and receive normal meta-messages becomes dulled. Communication becomes unreliable and unsuccessful. Attempts at humor may become dangerous.

Two people such as spouses cannot *not* communicate. Even silence says something! Dilemma: agreement cannot be reached —but disagreement cannot be tolerated. All choices are wrong! "I'll be damned if I do and damned if I don't." This is a nonsurvival, no-game condition. Concurrent emotions of fear, grief, anger and confusion can be sensed and felt by non-participants of all ages. These emotions are induced in children by the strong psychic fields or emotional vibrations of adults. If this is a daily experience, children may become unable to sense *or even imagine* love, security, fair play, common sense or serenity.

Perhaps vandalism and other antisocial acts are a desperate effort to reverse the flow, that is, to *cause* emotional reactions in others for a change, rather than being constantly overwhelmed by the crud being radiated by their parents.

Perhaps antisocial children have become addicted to the adrenalin which their system creates during the hectic scenes at home. Later, in the systematic serenity of school they may feel a letdown and need a fix, to be had by alarming or enraging an adult. At least it seems that kids do wild, destructive things because it feels good. There are other possible answers, of course. Some people resort to such means of communication as a last resort, since their more acceptable communication channels are jammed for various reasons. In a sense they are throwing a dandy tantrum. They are turning the tables by overwhelming the Establishment for a change. (See "Failing Big," p. 166.)

## FAMILY COUNSELING IS TRUE PREVENTIVE FIRST AID

Successful family counseling can ward off dozens of emotional crises and disasters, all of which are painful and very expensive in dollar cost. This is the way to go—there is no other way!

Family counseling is easily in the realm of amateur counseling:

—There is never any attempt at deep therapy.

—There is safety in numbers.

—In no ways playing doctor, the counselor is more of an interviewer, an information center, a referrer-to-higher-authority, or a referee for family squabbles.

—Hundreds of people in each community are partially qualified because they are already professionally trained: as teachers, lawyers, doctors, military officers and industrial supervisors. Given a short course and expert coaching, these people could help to work a tremendous improvement in divorces, welfare, dropouts, vandalism and crime.

## HOW CHILDREN LEARN

If a child lives with criticism he learns to condemn....
If a child lives with hostility he learns to fight....
If a child lives with fear he learns to be apprehensive....
If a child lives with pity he learns to feel sorry for himself....
If a child lives with ridicule he learns to be shy....
If a child lives with jealousy he learns what envy is....
If a child lives with shame he learns to feel guilty....

If a child lives with encouragement he learns to be confident....
If a child lives with tolerance he learns to be patient....
If a child lives with praise he learns to be appreciative....
If a child lives with acceptance he learns to like himself....
If a child lives with recognition he learns it is good to have a goal....
If a child lives with sharing he learns about generosity....
If a child lives with fairness he learns what justice is....
If a child lives with security he learns to have faith in himself....
If a child lives with friendliness he learns to be friendly....

If you live with serenity your child will live with peace of mind....

**WITH WHAT IS YOUR CHILD LIVING?**

CHAPTER 23

# Local Agencies

Where can you go for help? What kinds of help are available? How much will it cost? Few people could name more than a quarter of the agencies in their community. Besides learning where to ask for help, First Aiders need to know where to send people. Reviewing the list of local agencies may suggest to you an opportunity for volunteering your time and service. You could make new friends and help make your community a nicer place to live. Most folks are amazed to see how many people are working in careers designed to relieve the emotional suffering of others.

## PARTIAL LIST OF AGENCIES

Churches.

City and state police. The police sometimes sponsor recreational facilities and First Aid training classes, offer speakers for meetings, and so on.

Public-welfare office.

Vocational rehabilitation center. Career training for mentally and physically handicapped.

Alcoholics Anonymous.

Crisis clinic. In some cities this is a telephone service for helping a person find a professional counselor; a few cities have 24-hour clinics offering instant walk-in aid.

American Red Cross. Disaster aid; classes in First Aid, water safety and home nursing.

Boy Scouts; Girl Scouts.

Y.M.C.A.; Y.W.C.A. These organizations often sponsor hobby clubs, and a wide variety of classes and discussion groups.

Bureau of Indian Affairs.

Chamber of commerce; junior chamber of commerce.

City hostess; "Welcome Wagon."
Travelers Aid.
State employment office.
Mental-health center.
County health clinic.
Veterans' Affairs office.
U.S.O.
4-H Club; Future Farmers of America.
Health and Safety Council.
Foster homes for children.
Planned communities (farms) for the mentally retarded.
Salvation Army.
Good Will.
St. Vincent de Paul.
Social Security Administration.
Family counseling agency.
Social welfare office.
Boy's Club.
University extension services.
Kiwanis: most lodges sponsor a special social service.
Elks.
Moose.
Lions.
Odd Fellows.
American Legion.
Masons.
Knights of Columbus.
Eastern Star.
P. T. A.
Fire departments.
Nurses' organizations.
Parole board.
Library.
Office of Civil Defense.

CHAPTER 24

# Real Crises, Symptoms, Civil Disasters

In the opening chapter one reason for promoting Emotional First Aid was to teach people the signs of real trouble, the unmistakable symptoms which require fast, skillful attention and which warrant the trouble and expense of seeking immediate professional help.

Red Cross (physical) First Aid teaches the seriousness of such situations as uncontrolled bleeding, severe head injury, broken bones, severe burns, sharp pain in the stomach and angry red swelling. There are many others, of course.

Here are some of the emotional danger signs:

—Threats of destruction, to self or others.

—Unreasonable damage threatened or caused to valuable property, in rage or revenge, or for other "reason."

—An extended period of dizziness; loss of equilibrium.

—Sudden loss of memory.

—Sudden irrational behavior: doing very peculiar things, jabbering incoherently, hallucinating.

—Unrealistic fear of imaginary foes or situations.

—Frequent periods of deep depressions, incapacitating moods.

—Excessive, unexplained tiredness.

—Unexplained, uncontrolled weeping.

—Insomnia; nervousness.

—Frequent indigestion, sour stomach, heartburn.

—Sudden inability to make decisions; changing decisions unnecessarily; contradicting own statements.

## PROBLEMS IN GETTING HELP

If someone is badly burned or is crushed by a fall, he will cooperate in every way with efforts to get him a doctor. If he is rushed to a hospital, it is expected that someone there will start working on him within minutes or at least hours.

Not so with an emotional crisis. Very few people will help themselves to a psychiatrist or permit themselves to be taken by a spouse or fellow worker. It is virtually impossible for a spouse to get a mate to a psychiatrist when a home situation is heading toward divorce. In industry men quit good jobs in anger, and their bosses let them go, because people haven't been taught to recognize the symptoms of emotional shock and its implications.

But suppose there is an exceptional case. Suppose a man feels like he's on a bad trip, see. His buddy says: "Hey, man, you feel okay? You don't look too good. Let me take you to a shrink." So they start out, after first finding the name of a psychiatrist in the Yellow Pages. But what happens when he gets to the doctor's office? Instant couch? Negative. "Come back in three weeks." There are real cases where badly disturbed people were mature enough to seek emergency help at hospitals and clinics and none was available. The crisis-clinic program, such as it is, began in order to help desperate people get some sort of emergency care *now*.

Hopefully, Emotional First Aid will eventually convince the public that it is all right to seek professional emotional aid; in fact, that it is a good idea. Of equal importance, it is necessary to provide more aid stations and professional therapists. Remember, emotional shock must be treated *now,* or it will fade into the subconscious and become an engram, capable of causing emotional suffering for a lifetime.

## CAUSES OF EMOTIONAL CRISES

A crisis is a brink—a moment of decision when things either get better or get worse. A crisis is an opportunity for a disaster.

People's ability to withstand tribulation varies widely. What may be a routine problem or disappointment to some may be a near disaster for others less hardy. A family row may be a crisis; the fight may clear the air—or end in divorce.

Some causes of emotional crises:

# Real Crises, Symptoms, Civil Disasters

—Sudden loss of havingness (see chap. 7); sudden bad news.
—Death nearby, especially of loved ones; mangled bodies.
—Drugs, booze.
—Divorce and other types of legal actions.
—Very serious medical problems.
—Sudden unusual motion, lights, noise; imaginary danger.
—Crowd psychology, mass hysteria (induced panic).
—Psychological warfare; induced hopelessness and confusion.
—War, riots, raids; overwhelming brutality and destruction.
—Natural disasters: fire, flood, fierce storm, earthquakes, famine, drought, epidemic, volcanic eruption, shipwreck.

## TECHNICAL PROBLEMS

*Overwhelming odds.* When a disaster hits, you can't cop out and run. In a hurricane, flood or shipwreck you have to stay and make the best of it. Most people feel fearful panic when they realize, "This is for real! I may lose everything, even my life." We must remember, panic is a powerful, traumatic *emotion,* a scared *feeling,* which may do more actual harm than the real situation. Remember also, even when the situation seems hopeless, it isn't. Many people have pulled through "impossible" circumstances.

Panic scrambles your mind's computer. You can't think and solve problems if you lose your cool.

*Suddenness.* Most disasters catch us by surprise, unprepared. Most people don't know what is going on, not having studied case histories of similar events. Few people understand the physics of powerful events. There are invisible forces, various important time cycles, and predictable aftereffects.

*Trauma.* In a crisis everybody is in some degree of shock. Some will control themselves and do what needs to be done if possible. Others will fall apart and be unable to care for themselves and become an extra responsibility and burden to the more able. Remember, people in severe emotional shock are literally crazy for the moment. They may do *anything*—weird things—or nothing. They may drop the ball and fail in a critical task.

*Strong medicine.* Agonizing, superhuman decisions must be made during disasters. Grandma must be left behind in a flooded house; to take her would overload the small rowboat and all would perish. The forest fire is swooping down on a village; the last bus is only half full, but to wait for the stragglers who are laden with pets and keepsakes would cause all to perish. In a famine there may be food for dozens, not thousands; who is to play God? Or would it be better to share and share alike, and that all die? Student rioters demand the right to force vulgarity and destruction on a community in the name of freedom; what price is too high for unrestrained liberty? Who will dare to confront the dissenters and say, "This is it! Your freedom does not include the right to destroy the peaceful works of others. What you are doing is an infection which is capable of killing us all. You are an enemy to our civilized institutions. You yourselves admit it! Survival of our hard-won culture demands strong medicine!"

## WHAT YOU CAN DO

*Keep yourself at your best.* People who are physically and emotionally healthy, and well rested, generally face emergencies confidently. The strong healthy ones are the most likely to be willing and able to offer help.

*Have a personal plan.* What would you do if . . . ? What if your valley floods? What if the electric power fails for several hours or even days? Have you set aside some cash for a sudden trip? Are your vital papers in a safe, fireproof place? Do you have a list of all your household goods in the possession of a relative for use should your house burn down? Do you have spare gasoline and food?

*Join a local civil-defense group.* There are many voluntary organizations which exist to furnish community services *and pleasure,* for instance the Red Cross, Salvation Army, volunteer firemen, scouts, Civil Defense. Why join? (1) Teamwork counts. (2) Professional training is invaluable. (3) They have expensive specialized equipment; they need people like you to operate it. (4) They have experienced leadership for directing rescue operations. (5) Their leaders have the authority to give orders if necessary—to give the strong medicine. (6) You will have more fun studying courses and making plans and preparations with others of similar interest.

*Give (or take) standard training courses.* The way to have leaders when they are needed is to train them beforehand. The way to interest the public in Civil Defense is to teach them about it. There are good S.O.P. courses in leadership and Red Cross operations. Now you can offer a course in Emotional First Aid.

*Survival*: Know what the vital pieces are and hold them together at all cost!

## CHAPTER 25

# *Amateur Counseling*

One could construct a gradient scale of amateur counselors, rating them according to their efficiency in listening, advising, instructing, coaching, guiding and relieving suffering. The chart would certainly be colorful; it would include eight-year-olds playing doctor, sex advisers in the pool hall, Sunday-school teachers, bartenders, G.I. buddies in a barracks, scouters, cell mates in a penitentiary, schoolteachers, deans, pastors, nuns and personnel managers of large corporations.

For the purposes of this discussion, "amateur" counselor means all persons who are not psychologists, psychiatrists, ministers, priests or other professional counselors holding appropriate degrees and licenses. An amateur does not earn his living as a counselor. An amateur rating in no way defines or limits one's technical skill or understanding. There are amateur photographers and radio hams who are outstanding in their fields, and some amateurs have made notable contributions in techniques and inventions. Think for a moment of the athletes who compete in the Olympics; they are the world's finest—amateurs.

On the gradient scale of amateur counselors, this study is concerned with the top 10 percent, especially those who are already professionally trained as medical doctors, nurses, lawyers, teachers, military officers and industrial supervisors. Those people must counsel others in their daily work. With some additional training and study, and skillful coaching, those people could quadruple the available counseling hours in our nation in a year.

There are some of these people already living in each community, and their basic salary is already funded for. A few communities have already established "Family Services" clinics, using volunteer counselors and receptionists. We know it can be done because it *is* being done. A small city in British Columbia has a successful plan. Though office space was offered rent free in two of the churches and a legal office, it was decided to ensure independence from all religious and individual ties by renting a small suite in a modest downtown office building. It is not in a clinic; it is not in a church; it is not in the welfare building or city hall; you don't have to get a map and walk four blocks from the bus line; you usually don't need an appointment. And you don't need a lot of money, though modest fees are charged on the ability-to-pay basis to cover rent and telephone service. Cash contributions have been forthcoming from the chamber of commerce, several churches, the welfare department and some of the local lodges and service clubs. At one time there were three ministers, two lawyers, two social workers, one psychiatrist, two doctors and the director of a reform school on the counseling staff. Housewives took turns at the reception desk. These people are really doing something to reduce unnecessary emotional suffering!

## WHAT CAN AMATEUR COUNSELORS DO?

They can do everything! They can do whatever a highly paid psychiatrist could do for anyone who comes in and says, "I've got a bad problem and I don't know what I'm going to do."

1. Start a case-history record. Get the facts.
2. Listen. Listen. Listen.
3. Ask intelligent questions. Suggest new points of view.
4. Coach the person(s) on problem-solving techniques. Help him decide on a plan of action. Emphasize the importance of personal responsibility.
5. Refer him to a legal or medical specialist if necessary.
6. Make an appointment for another meeting.

If there should appear to be a need for drugs, deep therapy or physical restraint, the amateur counselor is certainly qualified to call for help, that is, either use the phone to locate a doctor or take the person to a hospital.

## FAILING BIG

People tend to equate Emotional First Aid with "emotional crisis." (Actually they are opposites.) People ask, "What could I possibly do to prevent someone from killing himself?"

Answer: Ask him why. He wants to tell you about this terrible problem that won't solve. Ask him to tell you. He is in shock; treat him for shock.

Killing oneself is failing big. It is a sort of ultimate weapon. So is quitting a good job mad, divorcing a decent wife, quitting school or going A.W.O.L. Each of us has a frustration breaking point. If that is reached, we seem to grasp control frantically, as if to demand a solution, all the while knowing that we can't have it our way. It is a kind of tantrum.

Failing big is dumping the chess board because you lost a piece. It spoils the game altogether.

Emotional First Aid teaches:

—Maintain the game at all costs. It's okay to lose sometimes.

—Good sportsmanship: Why be a sore loser?

—How to end cycles. Occasionally a desperate problem can be dissipated by simply asking, "What would happen if you decided that you didn't care about this problem? Could you tell yourself it really isn't all that important, then decide to drop it?"

—Problem-solving techniques.

—How to create new games.

—How to look past the desperately painful symptoms, to find the real problem.

—The importance of personal responsibility.

Morbid thoughts and threats of destruction do signal an emotional crisis. The person is in shock. (How this comes about and what can be done about it are detailed in chap. 9 on Emotional Shock.) People who contemplate failing big should be escorted to a crisis clinic if possible.

## NO DRUGS, NO DIRECT ORDERS

It is illegal and unwise to prescribe, administer, offer or recommend drugs or medicines to anyone unless you are a licensed doctor of medicine. If you as an amateur counselor firmly believe that a person needs medication or drugs, you must send him to a doctor. Exceptions are possible: in remote villages and camps, on ships and in disaster areas and war zones, nurses, Red Cross specialists and medical corpsmen may offer limited medication, following strict instructions.

Avoid giving direct orders to another person. (1) You can help him most by coaching him in making decisions for himself, thus accepting most of the responsibility for his actions. (2) If you don't give any direct advice, you can't give any *bad* advice, which might make you to blame for making matters worse. (3) A person in emotional shock can be expected to misinterpret your orders if you give any and to bungle the effort. You *can* coach him in making definite decisions, offer several ideas and perspectives, tell him about similar problems others had and how they were solved successfully.

There are several advantages, and some disadvantages, to group therapy, classes, workshops, seminars, discussions and "sharing." (1) The community can get more use out of a good counselor by using him to teach or coach ten or twenty people at once, rather than one at a time. (2) Members of a group may offer suggestions, insights or to-the-point questions which can be very helpful; a selected group having similar problems may be a valuable resource—Alcoholics Anonymous, for instance. (3) There is safety in numbers, both for the counselor and for the others. (4) Many people with emotional problems have a communication hangup; meeting with others would be a natural step toward re-establishing their self-confidence and willingness to have terminals.

Now, the problems. (1) There have been "sensitivity groups" where people have blurted out distasteful intimate bits which would better have remained bottled up until a private session could be arranged. Besides the long-lived embarrassment after the session, there have been reports of blackmail. Soul purging is not always good. (2) There are rules for successful group sessions, and the leader must insist that they be kept. Two important ones are: no one will preach or otherwise expound for more than a minute; and everyone should refrain from violent emotional displays, that is, from doing anything which would tend to stop the meeting.

## "STUDENTS: YOU ARE NOT PATIENTS"

Some of you are here because you have desperate personal problems. You have come to the right place, but—

This is not a good place to fall apart or let go.

We talk about and study certain kinds of emotional magic, *but we don't do it in class.*

You have some smarts or you wouldn't be here. For heaven's sake use it. Control yourself. Consider the problem if every student turned into a case. We expect your complete cooperation in this. Do not become a patient.

Yes, there is a small risk in the study of mental health. Almost everyone can recognize some of the symptoms in himself. Some of the lessons may actually stimulate severe discomfort. If this happens, don't panic. Consult the instructor after class.

These are the goals of this class.

—A working vocabulary, adequate theories.
—An introduction to self-analysis.
—An outline of emotional problems in our society.
—Simple Emotional First Aid procedures.
—Some basic philosophical principles.
—An introduction to special books.

## DANGERS IN COUNSELING BY AMATEURS

There are several hazards in counseling; some even apply to professional sessions. It is important for the patient to know something of these possibilities, for several reasons: (1) so that he won't be overcome with surprise or shock and perhaps be inclined to discontinue sessions abruptly; (2) so that he will not be unduly upset by wild tales he may hear from fellow students or patients; (3) so that he may gain more benefit from the sessions by observing developments more intelligently; (4) so that he will take more personal responsibility for his own welfare when out of session.

*Danger No. 1: Patient may be very suggestible.* Emotional First Aid may be little more than listening to a distraught person pour out his troubles. You can feed him, get him warm, offer quiet consolation and encouraging suggestions, perhaps direct him to official agencies. The danger at this stage is that he is very open to suggestions, almost like a hypnotized person. Some passing remark of yours may seem a very good idea, in fact the logical solution. Avoid giving direct advice. Help him consider all the facts. Try to keep in close touch for a few days. Encourage him to keep you advised of his plans and feelings *before* he does anything. Remind the patient at the end of each session that the session is over and he is on his own. Try to make sure that he is in present time and not in any sort of hypnotic trance. Avoid hypnotism of any kind at all times, and be alert to make certain that extra suggestibility doesn't occur accidentally. Emotional shock is a form of dangerous trance too. Try to see that no one leaves a session in a dangerous emotional condition which might impair driving or permit him to walk in front of an oncoming car.

*Danger No. 2: Patient may have a medical problem.* Counseling can never take the place of proper medical care, though it may make a person feel better for a while. There are several medical conditions which can make a person feel tired, discouraged, confused, fearful or sad. Malnutrition and lack of proper vitamins are common problems. Thyroid, diabetes, low blood pressure and toxicity should be considered. A serious medical condition might be overlooked too long by "positive thinking." It is possible that a person might have a heart or nervous condition which would make it unwise to risk the strain of deep therapy. If there is any doubt, the patient should get a good physical examination by a medical doctor.

*Danger No. 3: Interrupted sessions are very disturbing.* Emotional therapy requires that the patient's subconscious be bared in order to "see" hidden thoughts and fears. Here is a real Pandora's box. Weird effects can appear, visions, trances, sudden pain, deep grief, stark fear, rage. These are exactly what we are looking for, and notable case gains come from these experiences when properly dealt with. Permitting the session to stop during one of these effects can cause the patient severe discomfort and anxiety for hours or days. He may decide to cancel all therapy. He may even consider some drastic action—even perhaps suicide. This danger can be averted by (1) forewarning the patient; (2) continuing the procedure (question, command, process); keep doing the same thing until the effect subsides; *this is a must;* (3) building the patient's confidence and stamina before digging for dramatic incidents; (4) providing a secure environment free of disturbances; (5) arranging with the patient before commencing a session what you expect to do should the phone or doorbell ring; answer it very briefly, or ignore it.

*Danger No. 4: Wrong diagnosis.* Demanding that a non-religious person fall on his knees and pray that his sins be forgiven when his real problem seems to be whether to get a divorce might be an example of a wrong diagnosis. It might make matters worse! Freud taught that most personality troubles are caused by unfulfilled subconscious sex drives. We now know that there are many, many other types of aberration patterns besides sex. Understanding these other patterns gives us an intelligent choice and a better chance of perceiving the problem correctly.

*Danger No. 5: Breaking the code.* There are several interpersonal courtesies which are vitally important in counseling sessions. If you break the courtesy code, you blow the session and perhaps undo much good work. The counselor should know the code verbatim, must be drilled in exact compliance and must have a near-perfect self-control while his patient is weeping or raging. (The code is next, on p. 175.)

*Danger No. 6: Use of drugs.* The use or recommendation of drugs by lay counselors is forbidden by law and the code. There is a temptation to utilize tranquilizers, energizers, psycho-narcotics and stimulants. Drugs can be dangerous for several reasons: possible addiction, possible overdosage, possible fringe reactions, such

## Amateur Counseling

as causing an allergy or hallucination, possible loss of perspective and responsibility while under their influence.

Drugs tend to control a person's awareness and ability automatically. In contrast our goal is to cut through his automatic defenses and "psycho-shell," to help him achieve a satisfactory mature personality—not become a foggy robot.

*Danger No. 7: Mixed procedures.* A troubled mind can become more confused if more than one kind of therapy is attempted. Stay with the plan. Don't mix Christian Science, laying on of hands, confession of sins, yoga and hypnosis. These approaches seem to offer some satisfaction to some people. Mixing them creates too many variables for a lay counselor to be responsible for. Hypnosis is forbidden because of the danger of wild side effects. It is certainly not for amateurs.

*Danger No. 8: Overwhelming . . . swamping.* It is possible for a patient to get in over his head by trying to accomplish too much too soon. This makes his case worse instead of better. Knowing how to proceed at an optimum rate is vital to successful therapy, and much depends on a knowledge of the gradient scale, telltale signs and excellent theory.

Overwhelming can result when (1) there is a breakdown of ARC (communication, frankness) between counselor and patient; (2) session material is too weird and unrealistic; (3) the counselor forces an inaccurate evaluation on the patient; (4) patient is tired, hungry, sleepy or distracted by the environment; (5) he loses the games condition: perhaps he begins to feel that he can't do the process right or that he isn't pleasing the counselor or that he is stupid, guilty or hopelessly confused.

A patient who is overwhelmed is spinning his wheels. He may be sitting there, but he isn't doing the process. You might just as well stop, and begin again more gently.

Conversely, the counselor can become overwhelmed and saturated with other people's troubles, confusion and grief to the point where he loses his own courage and perspective. Occasional "faculty meetings" and advanced training classes will refresh him. Sometimes counselors have to be counseled to rid themselves of other people's troubles. This should not be necessary if they are counseling properly and successfully. Successful sessions should result in a sensation of deep satisfaction and a feeling of certainty about one's skill.

*Danger No. 9: Overt hostility.* Strangely, one reliable sign that a patient is improving is that he gets *mad enough to do something* about his situation. What he decides to do may not always agree with what others think he should do, or it may not be socially acceptable. He may blunder out of his shell into a hot frying pan! This may well be a step in the right direction, even though painful and awkward.

The danger here is that some anger may be turned toward his family, the clinic or the therapist. The counselor will be blamed for causing the effect or for failing to prevent it. He *is* responsible for (1) developing this stage gradually, (2) warning the patient and his family about this phenomenon, (3) teaching the patient suitable techniques for handling his hostilities and (4) helping him past this stage into greater emotional serenity and maturity.

The counselor should remember that some hostility toward the therapist is normal under certain conditions. It does not necessarily mean that he has made a serious social blunder, such as hurting or insulting the patient.

*Danger No. 10: False wings.* Can you imagine a hypnotist telling his subject, "You are now a big, powerful bird. Jump off the edge of this roof and fly"? Believing that he can fly will not satisfy aerodynamic requirements. Patients sometimes experience sudden wonderful release from inhibitions; they get vivid new goals and inspirations. There is some danger that they may go out and start projects they can't finish. The therapist may be blamed. Hours or days later there may come a contrasting letdown, during which the patient may feel discouraged about further sessions. It is unreasonable to expect therapy magic to transform black despondency into high-level buoyancy in one flashing leap. Ideally, successful therapy brings improvement in a controlled series of small increments during which the patient experiences cycles of wonderful relief and recurring blahs. He should soak up the delicious high and hang tight during the lows, knowing that it's okay and that he *is* getting better.

## PRE-SESSION ROUTINE

*Arrange the room.* Place your chairs close together. Close the door. Inquire about the patient's comfort: is the lighting okay? Is he warm enough?

*Present-time problem?* Has he eaten? If he's actually hungry, give him a light snack before starting. Does he have any other present-time problem? (A PT problem is one which seems urgent, distracting, enough to prevent full attention being focused on the session at hand.) A PT problem takes first priority over session plans.

*Sleepy?* Do not counsel past bedtime or too early in the morning if you or the patient is still drowsy. Avoid alcohol, tranquilizers or big meals before a session.

*Is he willing to be counseled?* Get his consent to submit to this business. Explain details of the session briefly; make certain he understands what you are trying to do and what is expected of him.

*Prearrange* about stopping time, interruptions, phone calls, etc.

*Explain the importance of discipline* during the session. He must stay in session, especially during boredom or discomfort. Mention the "Don't stop till we're through" rule. Avoid side remarks and chitchat.

*Personality clashes?* Do you remind him of someone? Does one of your physical features or mannerisms annoy him? If so, handle as a PT problem, immediately.

*Goal for the session?* Help him decide what he wants and what he expects you to do for him. Create a "We're going to work this out together" atmosphere.

*Remarks, reports* or *complaints* about previous sessions, classes or other types of therapy? Confront the hangups and blow them.

*First-time introduction.* Being counseled is a new, very personal experience. People should be given some warning of what to expect and some special instructions such as "Foolishness at first usually makes sense at the end," "It's okay for you to get strange impressions and emotions," "What turns on an effect will turn it off again, if continued."

## PATIENT'S CODE

*Come prepared* for a session. Be prompt. Be rested. Eat first. It's okay to have a cup of coffee for extra alertness, but two cups may demand an unnecessary "pit stop" in the middle of something critically important. If you have been sitting or studying, wash your face, stretch and get some fresh air before going to sit another hour.

*Expect a wonderful experience.* You may learn something or change an attitude which could brighten your whole life. Welcome strong medicine. If tears, anger, fear or even physical pain turns on, report it to your counselor and *keep going*. Face whatever comes; *do not try to stop*. This is how big gains are made. Your counselor will see you through to complete relief.

*Be willing to follow directions.* The finest counseling skills will be wasted if you are not willing to do your part.

*Do your homework cheerfully.* If you are assigned reading and writing exercises, do them. You will be studying facts of life that you need to know. Your happiness and success depend on understanding.

*Do your part, or pay your way.* There is a natural law that you can't get much for nothing. In order for you to value something highly, you must exchange something of nearly equal value for it. "Return the flow," "You will get out what you put in," etc. Free counseling is seldom valued by the patient. Expect to pay, for your own good. If you are really short of cash, consider trading your time and services (working it out); or sign a promissory note for a fair fee. This is not a money-making scheme; it is a natural requirement for good two-way communication.

*Acknowledge a success.* If you achieve one or more of your session goals, if you feel better, or have gained some understanding (cognition), tell your counselor so. If you think he is taking a very personal interest in you and is doing a good job of counseling, tell him. Remember, a communication cycle isn't complete until it is acknowledged. Following the same logic, you are permitted to feed back your feelings and views about negative impressions too. It is a handicap to both of you if you go away annoyed about something. End cycles and clear the air after each session.

## COUNSELOR'S CODE

*Perform pre-session routine.* Remember, you are about to communicate with a subconscious mind—a stranger, even though the patient is an old friend. Formalities and common courtesy are very important.

*Maintain a professional attitude.* Refuse to process or accept money from anyone unless you honestly believe you can help him. Keep all appointments. Never get angry. Avoid sympathizing with the patient. Don't become emotionally involved, but take a personal interest in his safety and progress.

*Never evaluate.* Never explain why such a thing happened. Don't explain significances or meanings. Don't give direct advice about his personal matters. He *must* figure them out himself.

*Never invalidate.* Never question or correct your patient, no matter how silly, crazy, immoral or false his story may seem to you.

*Keep secrets.* You will be trusted with many intimate details. *Never* discuss them with anyone.

*Stay in session.* Keep at the process; don't stop to chitchat or compare notes. Don't let the patient become confused or stuck on a dilemma. Don't ask questions he can't answer. Don't *you* turn on something from your case. Keep alert—counsel every minute.

*Never walk away* during a session. Don't answer the phone, don't get a drink, don't light a cigarette. You open a mind during a session much as a surgeon opens a body during an operation. Don't leave until you close properly. A session is not a friendly visit; it is serious business—and may be a life-and-death matter.

*Don't let him leave.* Never permit the patient to walk out or otherwise disrupt the session. Every com lag or charged incident must be flattened or run out by the continued use of the same process, question or command, even though severe discomfort may turn on while doing so. Don't be "kind" to someone by letting him quit in the middle of an engram.

*Avoid confusion.* Seek the patient's level of reality. Don't snow him. Maintain good ARC at all costs. Don't change processes abruptly or in mid-cycle. Avoid changing counselors if possible.

*End each session systematically.* Review events of the session; list case gains; clearly restate "where we stand," and list some things the patient can do for himself between sessions. Make certain that the patient is back in present time enough to be fully responsible for his physical welfare after he leaves the office.

**CHARLES R. STURGE**
3044 Kaiser Rd. N.W. #3
Olympia, WA 98502